V

2002

For Beth and Phil, with much love.
Have a very happy life together!

Most authors can only dream of being part of a successful publishing team producing a series of best-selling books, so I consider myself extremely lucky to be working with everyone at Constable & Robinson for a fifth year. Five years! It seems like only yesterday . . . As ever, it's been a pleasure to produce these books in tandem with Nicola Chalton, Nova Jayne Heath and Nick Robinson. Many thanks as well to Elaine Henderson for managing the project and special thanks to Jane Horwood for all her eagle-eyed editing skills, to Annie Lionnet for her wonderful back-up, to Bill Martin for his superstar qualities and to Chelsey Fox for being a super agent. What a team!

VIRGO
2002

Jane Struthers

This is a Parragon Book
First published in 2001

Parragon
Queen Street House
4 Queen Street
Bath BA1 1HE
UK

Produced by Magpie Books, an imprint of
Constable & Robinson Ltd, London

Illustrations courtesy of Slatter-Anderson, London

ISBN 0-75255-704-1

A copy of the British Library Cataloguing-in-Publication Data
is available from the British Library

Printed and bound in the EC

CONTENTS

Sun Sign Dates for 2002

Virgo 24 August – 23 September

Libra 24 September – 23 October

Scorpio 24 October – 22 November

Sagittarius 23 November – 21 December

Capricorn 22 December – 20 January

Aquarius 21 January – 18 February

Pisces 19 February – 20 March

Aries 21 March – 20 April

Taurus 21 April – 21 May

Gemini 22 May – 21 June

Cancer 22 June – 22 July

Leo 23 July – 23 August

INTRODUCTION

Dear Virgo

Are you ready for a fabulous 2002? With the help of my astrological guide to the year, you'll be able to make the most of the benefits coming your way and steer around any possible pitfalls.

So what have I got lined up for you in this year's book? **Virgo 2002** kicks off with a summary of what the year will bring for you in your relationships, health, money and career. After that comes your day by day guide to 2002, complete with at-a-glance charts for each month so you can get an idea of what's in store for you.

Your Virgo Sun Sign tells you all sorts of fascinating information about yourself, including the way you handle your relationships, money, health and career. After that comes **Love and the Stars**, telling you how each sign gets along with all the other signs in the zodiac. You can start by reading all about your relationships and then you can discover how the other signs get on with you. If you want an instant assessment of how a relationship will work out, I've included two handy charts for you, so you can easily see how you fare with other signs for love and sex, and also for friendship.

In **Your Potential and Creativity**, you can read about ways to express your sign's unique potential. These could introduce you to a new hobby and they might even lead you into a new career.

If you were born at the beginning or end of Virgo and you aren't sure which sign you belong to, you'll love reading **Born on the Cusp?** because it will clear up the mystery at long last!

Have fun reading this book, and have a wonderful 2002!

Jane Struthers

THE YEAR 2002

Friends and Lovers

If you're hoping to read some good news, here it is! Friends will be a fantastic addition to your life in 2002. Some of these are chums who you know already, but others are people who haven't entered your life yet. You'll be meeting them during the coming year, and especially in the first seven months of 2002.

If you're wondering how you're going to meet all these friends because you don't have many opportunities to make new pals, then you need to widen your horizons a little. Budding mates are unlikely to come knocking on your door! Consider joining a club or society that caters for one of your interests, so you'll already have something in common with the people you meet. That should help to break the ice a little! Volunteering to do some charity work will introduce you to new faces, and will also make you feel you're doing your bit to help society. If you're confined to home for some reason or you don't like the groups in your area, how about getting involved in something over the Internet? Or you might consider joining a national organization that has local meetings. Keep trying until you find something you like!

Family relationships have been slightly fraught over the

past couple of years, and you may still be going through the mill with certain members of the clan. Domestic and family difficulties may be dogging your footsteps in 2002 if your birthday falls between 6 and 12 September. You might be worried about someone's health or have to steel yourself to the idea of one of your children moving away from home. Do your best to find ways round these problems, or to alter your attitude to circumstances if they are inevitable.

Health

Health is always an important topic for you. If you're a typical Virgo you like to keep yourself in as good a condition as possible. You also tend to worry when things seem to be going wrong.

In 2002, there will be times when your health seems erratic and difficult to predict. Your energy levels may go up and down like a yo-yo, so you feel fantastic one day and listless the next. You may also become rather nervy and restless every now and then, and perhaps have bouts of insomnia or indigestion. These are all indications that you need to introduce more variety into your daily routine, and also that you may be allowing yourself to become too het up and tense. Try to find a relaxation technique that doesn't take up a lot of time and which can become a daily habit. Sticking to a moderate, healthy diet will also help to combat mood swings and sleepless nights.

Worrying won't help, either. If you're a born worrier and it's making a misery of your life, vow that this is the year you'll do something about it. How about buying a book that will help you to get things more in proportion? Or maybe you'd prefer to control your worrying by limiting your fretting time to five minutes each day and then deliberately switching off and thinking about something else? What seems like a monumental effort at first may soon become second nature. There might even be days when you forget to worry at all!

Money

Will you be feeling flush in 2002 or will you be counting every penny? That depends mostly on the direction that your career takes. There's been a lot of activity in this area of your life in recent years and it isn't over yet. So if you already know that your job may not last for much longer or you're currently looking for work, it will make sense to save as much money as possible. Otherwise you may be left high and dry at the wrong moment. Following on from this, it might be a good idea to put aside a little money every month, if you have it, for a rainy day. If that rainy day doesn't happen, you'll have a fun fund instead!

It looks as though promotion or a better-paid job might be on the cards in 2002, which is good news. You might also consider making some money from a favourite hobby – could someone pay you to do something that you currently do for pleasure? It could be the start of a very profitable enterprise and eventually it might even turn into a full-time job.

Career

You belong to one of the most practical and efficient signs of the zodiac, and this is a year to remind everyone of that fact. This doesn't mean working yourself into the ground until you become exhausted. It means doing your best work and showing yourself in a good light, so influential people will take notice of you.

If you've been toiling away for years now, without much to show for it in the way of thanks or job prospects, all that may change in 2002. You may find that you have the backing of a boss or superior who wants to give you the rewards you so obviously deserve. Or if you suspect hell would freeze over before that happened, how about taking the initiative and signing up with an employment agency? You might be astonished by the difference it makes and the prospects that are opened up for you. If you want to look for a new job in 2002 and are wondering when the best time would be, consider making a move in early June when you'll get the benefits of the Eclipsed New Moon. It should be a brilliant time to make a fresh start in your career!

It's a good idea to take a look at your regular routine this year. If you're getting fed up with the pattern of your days, do something to change them. Even minor amendments could make you feel better, so don't imagine it has to be all or nothing.

Your Day by Day Guide

JANUARY AT A GLANCE

Love	♥ ♥ ♥ ♥ ♥
Money	£ $ £
Career	💻 💻
Health	☼ ☼ ☼ ☼ ☼

• *Tuesday 1 January* •

You're all ready for a fantastic 2002! You're starting the New Year in exactly the right mood because you're feeling optimistic and confident. Even if you were up half the night celebrating you won't let that put you off your stroke for long. An ideal way to spend the day is to be with some of your favourite people. But you should also spare the time to jot down some New Year resolutions while your outlook is so expansive and positive.

• *Wednesday 2 January* •

Get to grips with anything that's been worrying you lately. Rather than let it prey on your mind you'll feel far more in control of your life if you can take some positive action. You'll also be glad that you set the ball rolling. If you're fretting about something that can't be altered, it will help to tell a loved one about it. You may also realize that if you can't change the situation you need to alter your attitude towards it in some way.

• *Thursday 3 January* •

Who said the party season was over? You're only interested in enjoying yourself today, preferably in the company of someone who always makes your knees go weak. If that isn't possible, then go for a night on the tiles with some friends. You never know who you might meet in the process! Watch out if you're visiting the sales because it could be an expensive trip, especially if you see something that is luxurious or extravagant. You've just got to have it!

• *Friday 4 January* •

Someone loses their cool today and gets in a bit of a state. This could easily lead to a row because they aren't thinking about what they're saying and that's a sure-fire way to put someone's nose out of joint. Unfortunately, you could easily be the person who ends up with steam coming out of their ears. If you're angry about something try to calm down long enough to work out whether it's worth causing such a ruckus.

• *Saturday 5 January* •

You're in a very industrious and organized mood today. It's a marvellous chance to catch up with any chores that have been overlooked recently because you've had more exciting things to do. This is also a good day to talk to people who are older or wiser than you because they could have some good ideas, especially when it comes to making your money work for you. Even so, bear in mind that they may err on the side of caution.

• *Sunday 6 January* •

Feelings run high today and they could easily spill over into tears and tantrums. It won't help if someone is feeling insecure at the moment because that may make them possessive or reluctant to let you out of their sight. So much togetherness will quickly grate on your nerves and the result will be inflammatory. Thrash out your differences but try to stick to the facts so you don't get sidetracked by past grievances.

• *Monday 7 January* •

It's another day when tempers are short. This time it's because familiarity is breeding contempt, so be very careful when you're around people you know inside out. Their funny little habits will soon have you gritting your teeth with irritation – and they may react in exactly the same way towards you! It will all add up to a lot of hot air unless you can control your annoyance.

• *Tuesday 8 January* •

Thank goodness the atmosphere is much better today. Everyone has calmed down after yesterday's outbursts and you're ready to put the entire experience behind you. It will be good if you can show there are no hard feelings. If you're wondering which is the best day to go out on the town this week, it's today! You're in exactly the right mood to let your hair down in the company of someone special or a group of friends.

• *Wednesday 9 January* •

If you're a typical Virgo you pride yourself on your grasp of the facts and your ability to concentrate on practicalities. So you'll soon feel frustrated and annoyed with yourself today when you struggle to keep your mind on anything for long. It keeps straying off on to other subjects and you're easily distracted. If possible, delay any detailed work until tomorrow and concentrate instead on activities that use your imagination. Much to your delight, you'll find you excel.

• *Thursday 10 January* •

If you couldn't concentrate yesterday, you're back on form today. Even better, you're able to make up for lost time by focusing on things with precision. Grab the chance to check what you did yesterday just to make sure you didn't overlook anything important or make some embarrassing slip-ups. If you've got to fill in a form or read the small print of an agreement at some point, do it today while your mind is razor-sharp. You'll soon spot any snags.

• *Friday 11 January* •

You're very quick on the draw today but your hair-trigger responses could land you in hot water, especially if you act without thinking. The trouble is that you're easily irritated and don't have any patience for slowcoaches. You think they're holding you back and will probably say so, whether it's true or not. There could also be a family dispute to contend with when someone speaks out of turn or is too defensive for words. Oh dear!

• *Saturday 12 January* •

You're in the mood to have some fun today! Get together with some of your favourite people and do something that you'll all enjoy. How about trying something new, such as visiting a restaurant or club that you've never been to before? If you're hoping to meet someone new this year, what happens now gives you plenty of confidence about your powers of attraction. Someone makes it plain that they're interested in you, but are you so keen on them?

• *Sunday 13 January* •

Love and happiness are the main highlights of the coming two weeks, thanks to today's New Moon. Don't be surprised if you're in great demand socially. Or maybe you're the one who'll be issuing the invitations? A new love affair might brighten up your life now or you could enjoy a renaissance with your current partner. If you can spare the time, how about starting a creative project that could lead on to greater things?

• *Monday 14 January* •

Try not to spend too much time by yourself today because that will be depriving everyone of your wonderful company! This is one of those glorious days when people are full of praise for you and they can't get enough of you. It may only be Monday but you're in the mood to go out on the town. You're also drawn to the sales and tempted by the thought of buying yourself some flattering new clothes.

• *Tuesday 15 January* •

You have a good eye for detail today. However, it's important that you know when to stop otherwise you'll get bogged down in facts and will end up feeling exhausted. You may also struggle to see the wood for the trees. If this happens, take a short breather and get some fresh air. When you come back you'll find it easier to keep things in perspective. If there have been problems with a colleague, this is a good chance to talk about what's gone wrong.

• *Wednesday 16 January* •

Be prepared! Some irritating disruptions are on their way and you'll need plenty of patience to get through them. If you're at work you may have to deal with someone who keeps interrupting you or has some weird ideas that you think are totally impractical. At least it will keep life interesting – there's a chance that you're feeling bored with your current routine and are looking for ways to liven things up.

• *Thursday 17 January* •

A certain person has a very powerful way of getting their point across today and they don't seem to mind how heavy-handed they are in the process. You may end up feeling as though you're being bullied into submission, especially if they use a little emotional blackmail to get their own way. It's hard to deal with them when they're in this mood and you aren't keen to let them triumph with their current tactics. Sounds like stalemate!

• *Friday 18 January* •

Life takes on an all-or-nothing quality from today. Over the next few weeks you won't be very interested in doing things that have little meaning for you. You certainly won't see the point of doing something for the sake of it, especially where your finances and sex life are concerned. However, if you want to put a tricky situation to rights, this is when you'll really come into your own and see some results.

• *Saturday 19 January* •

If you've got your eye on a certain person, this is a marvellous day to make your move. After all, nothing ventured, nothing gained! Take things gently and use subtle tactics rather than throwing yourself at this person. If you're at work you'll enjoy the rapport between you and colleagues. There might even be a hint of sexual attraction between you and a workmate. Is this the start of something big?

• *Sunday 20 January* •

Over the next four weeks you'll get a lot of satisfaction out of being of service to people. You'll want to do the best you can for them, regardless of whether it's part of your job. Even so, if your job is in one of the service industries you'll want to channel all your energies into it now. It's also a good opportunity to take better care of your health, which is always an abiding interest for a Virgo like you.

• *Monday 21 January* •

Watch out for a tricky atmosphere today. If you're at work it will be difficult to keep on the right side of colleagues and customers. Someone may be expecting you to do more than your fair share of the workload, especially if they seem to be taking you for granted at the same time. If you want some time off this isn't the best day to ask for it because you may not get the answer you were hoping for. Can you delay the request for a few days?

• *Tuesday 22 January* •

It's another day when people are operating on a short fuse and it may be for exactly the same reasons as yesterday. Unfortunately it will be tempting to blurt out a few home truths to someone without thinking them through first, which could lead to a free and frank exchange of views. You may also have to mind your Ps and Qs when talking to someone who's very sensitive or who monitors every utterance so they can attack any politically incorrect ideas. Boring!

• *Wednesday 23 January* •

Have a think about your career and job prospects today. Are you happy with the way things are going or do you fancy a change? If you're interested in the idea of branching out in new directions, consider what these might be. Ideally, you should do something that combines your past experiences and qualifications with something excitingly new and different. And if there's something you've always wanted to try, is there some way to turn that dream into reality now?

• *Thursday 24 January* •

You're feeling confident and pleased today, especially when it comes to the way you perform at work. There's such a strong focus on your job this week that you want to do it as well as possible. It's a lovely excuse to get friendly with a colleague now, so find some way of breaking the ice with them. You may also be kept busy looking after the welfare of a workmate or customer. It's a busy but satisfying day.

• *Friday 25 January* •

It's unlike you to be so idealistic but you've definitely got stars in your eyes today and your feet are floating several inches above the floor. You only want to believe the best of people and are quite prepared to close your eyes to their misdemeanours.

Unfortunately that could mean you're ignoring someone's glaring faults or errors. You may also have to deal with someone who thinks they're behaving like a saint but who is really on a massive ego trip. Make sure you don't fall into this trap yourself!

• *Saturday 26 January* •

If you're at work or in contact with a colleague today, use your charm to get out of any hot water. You'll soon be able to talk your way out of prospective trouble and into their good books. Even if you aren't trying to save your bacon you simply can't help charming the pants off someone right now. Whether you take that literally is up to you, of course!

• *Sunday 27 January* •

This is a marvellously productive day and you'll end it with a real sense of achievement. It's terrific if you want to concentrate on a current task because you'll manage that with no trouble at all. This is also a good opportunity to pick someone's brains and ask their advice, provided you remember that their opinions will be rather cautious and conservative. Don't expect this person to encourage you to take risks.

• *Monday 28 January* •

Virgos are born worriers. If you're the sort of Virgo who's carrying on that tradition then you need to act carefully over the next two weeks. If something is bugging you at the moment, it's no good stewing about it. Instead, you need to take constructive action, even if it's only the first step on a very long journey. The simple fact that you've done something to help yourself will soon make you feel better.

• *Tuesday 29 January* •

You're in a rather sentimental and emotional mood today, although you'll prefer to keep your feelings to yourself rather than share them with all and sundry. You might decide to shut yourself away and look through some treasured keep-sakes and mementoes. It's also a lovely day for being with some of your nearest and dearest, even if all you do is share a meal and have a relaxing time in front of the television.

• *Wednesday 30 January* •

Someone seems to have lit a fire under you today because you're full of energy and eager to get things done. You've also got an ambitious streak now, which is just what you need if you're keen to get your name in lights. If you want to persuade a prospective employer or superior that you're the right candidate for the job, your current quiet determination and single-minded approach will work wonders.

• *Thursday 31 January* •

It won't take much to catch you on the raw today and make you suspicious of someone's motives. It doesn't help that you're feeling rather defensive so will instantly rise to the bait if someone seems to be getting at you. What's more, you're taking things quite seriously and may make a meal out of incidents that you'd usually shrug off. Ask yourself what's wrong and how you can make things better.

FEBRUARY AT A GLANCE

Love	♥ ♥ ♥ ♥ ♥
Money	£ $
Career	💻 💻 💻 💻 💻
Health	☼ ☼ ☼ ☼ ☼

• *Friday 1 February* •

You want to put your heart and soul into whatever you do today. You're not interested in half-measures or seeing how much you can get away with. Take note of what happens at work and when dealing with members of the family because you might have a rather emotional encounter with someone that makes you view them in a new light. They might also offer to get you out of a jam or give you some moral support. What a nice start to February!

• *Saturday 2 February* •

The good atmosphere continues today, when once again you find it easy to get on with colleagues and customers. This is also a good day to spend your money on items that will boost your health or fitness. You might decide to invest in some vitamin or mineral supplements, you could buy a book that outlines a new health regime or you may be inspired to enrol in a gym or leisure centre.

• *Sunday 3 February* •

Someone pushes your patience to the limit today and it won't take much to make you snap. This is especially likely if you're already feeling tired, edgy or fraught, because your frazzled nerves will soon make you over-react. If you're rushing around trying to do several things at once because you're running out of time, you'll need more haste and less speed if you want to avoid becoming a butterfingers or getting yourself into a right old state.

• *Monday 4 February* •

Over the next few days it won't always be easy to keep in touch with loved ones. Some of them may never be around when you try to contact them or it may be impossible to reach them because their phone is on the blink. If you're currently trying to organize a forthcoming social event or celebration, rather than battle with crossed wires over the next few days it may be less frustrating to put everything on hold until Friday and then to carry on where you left off.

• *Tuesday 5 February* •

Are you in the mood for some shopping? You're certainly keen to escape from your usual Tuesday routine and do something a little different for a change. A visit to a nearby town or city will soon pep you up, and it's even better if you can take someone along for company. If you decide to spend money you'll be drawn to items that enable you to keep in touch with others, such as a new phone or computer. Even so, it might be a good idea to delay buying anything until Friday, to avoid possible problems with faulty goods.

• *Wednesday 6 February* •

Take stock of your current health regime. If you've been trying to get yourself in better shape, how are you coming along? Can you see any progress yet? If not, maybe it's time to rope in some expert advice? This is also a good day to think about your domestic routine. Can you think of any changes that will save you time or be more productive? Ask everyone concerned before you put your ideas into action, though, to make sure they're in agreement with you.

• *Thursday 7 February* •

If you're at work today, be prepared for some interesting surprises. For instance, you might meet someone who exerts a magnetic attraction for you, even if you're already part of a happy couple. If this happens you'll be very torn about what to do next. Should you just have a harmless flirtation with this new person, should you try to put them out of your mind, or should you let your heart rule your head? It won't be as easy a decision as you imagine.

• *Friday 8 February* •

Communications start to get back to normal today, which is good news if you've been waiting impatiently for the all-clear before continuing with your social arrangements or buying that gadget you've got your eye on. You might even receive a backlog of post in the next couple of days. Any decisions that you take now about your love life will have a powerful impact, so don't rush into hasty conclusions if you aren't sure about them.

• *Saturday 9 February* •

A certain someone seems to have a black cloud hanging over their head and they're in a very bad mood. The more closely involved you are with this person, the more likely it is that you'll get the rough edge of their tongue. Great! There could also be a falling-out with someone over a social event, especially if they feel they've been left out or they don't want you to go out without them. If you give as good as you get, it will be quite a rumpus.

• *Sunday 10 February* •

If your nerves are still feeling frayed after yesterday's altercations, settle down with the Sunday papers or a favourite book and let the rest of the world pass you by. You'll enjoy giving your brain a good workout now, so how about pitting your wits against a crossword, puzzle or competition? You'll enjoy the mental challenge. If you haven't spoken to a loved one in ages, get on the phone or write them a letter.

• *Monday 11 February* •

Any changes that you make today will have far-reaching consequences and they'll also work out very well. Provided, that is, you've taken everyone's views and needs into account and you aren't simply doing what you want. A little cooperation and consultation go a long way now so don't ignore the benefits of working as part of a team. Areas to concentrate on for maximum success are joint finances, your sex life, your home and your family.

• *Tuesday 12 February* •

The next few weeks are a marvellous chance to improve your one-to-one relationships. There will be much more harmony with other people than usual, helped by your eagerness to keep everyone happy. However, although it's a good idea to meet people halfway rather than insist on getting what you want, try to resist the idea that you should be too accommodating or even ignore your own needs. Is it a case of peace at any price?

• *Wednesday 13 February* •

Things don't go entirely according to plan at work today. Someone could do things that take you by surprise or they might reveal an unexpected side to their character. This may be a mixed blessing because although it keeps life interesting it will also mean you have to think on your feet. If you've arranged a business meeting or job interview for today, there could be some last-minute interruptions or changes of plan.

• *Thursday 14 February* •

It may be Valentine's Day but it seems that someone isn't entering into the spirit of things. They may be in a sulk or simply determined to take their bad mood out on you. Or maybe you're the one who's scowling fit to bust? Don't despair because you can still rescue the situation, provided you're prepared to clear the air first. This could be tricky at the time but it will make a huge difference to the mood of the day. Besides, think of the fun you'll have kissing and making up!

• *Friday 15 February* •

Extravagance is your big bugbear today. Money will slip through your hands like sand, given half the chance. To make matters worse, it may be the joint account that you're dipping into! If you take a friend along with you to the shops, don't expect them to exercise any restraint either. They may even encourage you to spend more money! The best way to handle this is either to leave your credit cards at home or only take the cash that you're prepared to spend. Once that's gone, your shopping spree is over.

• *Saturday 16 February* •

It's a day to enjoy yourself! This is exactly the excuse you need to let your hair down so try to make sure you do something enjoyable at some point in the day. Ideally, you should grab your other half or a good friend by the hand and whisk them off to a favourite restaurant or somewhere else that you like visiting. If you're setting off for a weekend break then you'll have a marvellous time. It will be such fun that you'll wonder why you don't do it more often.

• *Sunday 17 February* •

Relax and take life easy whenever you get the chance today. It will do you the world of good to unwind and catch your breath. If there's no escaping some work, get it out of the way sooner rather than later so you don't have it hanging over you. You're feeling very considerate right now and if someone needs your help you'll be at their side in a flash. It might help if you can do some shopping or housework for them.

• *Monday 18 February* •

There seems to be a great divide between you and a loved one today. You feel distant from one another and it's not a very comfortable experience. You may even be physically separated, perhaps because duty had to come before pleasure. Unfortunately, you may also be wondering whether this relationship is going to last. However, you should only do something drastic if you're absolutely convinced that it's the best thing for all concerned. Don't break up with someone simply because you're feeling lonely or neglected.

• *Tuesday 19 February* •

Relationships become an even bigger focus for you from today. During the next four weeks you'll place so much importance on your partnerships that your sense of identity will be affected by them. You'll feel much more confident and happy when you're with other people than when you're by yourself. It's a terrific chance to get involved in some form of team work because you'll pull out all the stops to make sure it's a success.

• *Wednesday 20 February* •

Keep your head down today if you want a nice, quiet life. Otherwise you'll be faced with lots of flak from people who are looking for a fight or who want to abuse their current position of power. You might also have a disagreement with an older friend or relative who you're convinced is throwing their weight around. Both of you are determined to stand your ground so it will be stalemate, with neither of you budging an inch.

• *Thursday 21 February* •

You're in a very businesslike mood today, which is great if you were distracted by yesterday's events and have a lot of catching up to do. You're very keen to make the most of your time so why not plan your schedule in advance? That way, you can avoid doing things twice or tackling them in the wrong order. Someone in authority may have some words of advice for you but you'll think they're rather dull or depressing.

• *Friday 22 February* •

You're in a really good mood today! You'll manage to get on well with everyone you encounter, so it's great for making a favourable impression on someone. Although you'll do well if you're at work, you'll really come into your own when you're with friends and partners. It's a terrific excuse to go out on the town with some of the gang. And if you're taking part in a group activity you may find yourself basking happily in the spotlight.

• *Saturday 23 February* •

Make the most of today's industrious and organized mood. You're really skilled at marshalling your thoughts now so it would be a shame to let an opportunity like this pass you by. Even if you weren't intending to do any work today it could be worth your while to change your plans and tackle paperwork, write letters or fill in forms. Your brain is working so well you'll take pleasure in sorting everything out and making sure you've done things properly.

• *Sunday 24 February* •

Allow your imagination full rein today, especially if you're looking for ways to relax. You'll find it far easier to come up with creative ideas than to tackle subjects that call for concentration and an eye for detail. If you're interested in using the power of your mind to improve your health, do some research into creative visualization, self-healing and meditation. You're very receptive to these ideas now and you'll also be very good at them.

• *Monday 25 February* •

Your idea of heaven today is to hide away from the madding crowd with a very select group of people. You may only want to be with your nearest and dearest, or you might even decide that the only company you want is your own. You'll certainly benefit from this mini retreat, especially if you can do things that mean a lot to you but may not have much importance for anyone else.

• *Tuesday 26 February* •

Someone's got an axe to grind and they seem to be sharpening it with you in mind. If a loved one or partner has been storing up resentments or grievances, they'll let them all out today. Try not to let yourself get sucked into this person's manipulative mood because they'll do their level best to make you dance to their tune. They may also try to use money to make you do what they want. Keep out of their way whenever possible and don't be afraid to stand up for yourself.

• *Wednesday 27 February* •

Today's Full Moon is urging you to think carefully about your life over the next two weeks. If you want to make some changes to your world, now is the time to swing into action. You're determined to improve your situation and the Full Moon will give you its backing. Take a deep breath and be prepared to jettison anything that is no longer valid in your life or which you only cling to because it's a habit. Smoking, drinking or a destructive relationship might all go by the wayside over the coming weeks. It's a liberating thought.

• *Thursday 28 February* •

Relationships go well today. In fact, you'll feel left out if you have to spend too long by yourself. Ideally, you want to be with people who mean a lot to you, but if they aren't around you should still join forces with someone. If you're currently feeling dissatisfied with a relationship because it doesn't have much emotional depth, ask yourself whether you're contributing as much to it as you think it deserves. Don't rush to lay all the blame at the feet of the other person!

MARCH AT A GLANCE

Love	♥ ♥ ♥ ♥ ♥
Money	£ $ £ $ £
Career	💻 💻
Health	☼ ☼ ☼ ☼

• *Friday 1 March* •

Your instincts usually tell you to be cautious but from today you're tempted to take a few risks! The next six weeks are a wonderful opportunity to branch out in new directions and to accept the challenges that come along. Travel looks especially good now because you're in the mood to visit somewhere for the first time. You're also ready to abandon any fears or restrictions that have been holding you back recently and to live a little.

• *Saturday 2 March* •

Once again you're in an intrepid mood but try not to go overboard otherwise you'll end up doing something you regret. It's very tempting to push yourself to the limit now because you're impatient with anything and anyone that threatens to tie you down. You may even want to turn this into a battle of wills with someone, setting yourself up against them. If you do that, you can expect to have a big row on your hands.

• *Sunday 3 March* •

This is a fantastic day for thinking things through very carefully. Yesterday's daredevil mood has evaporated, leaving you in a much more phlegmatic and rational frame of mind. Topics to contemplate include anything connected with your home and family, and also anything linked with your work and daily routine. It's marvellous for getting down to the nitty-gritty of a subject and considering it from every angle.

• *Monday 4 March* •

Your social life looks good today. It seems that certain people can't get enough of you and they're clamouring for your attention. You might receive a lovely phone call from someone or an invitation that's far too good to turn down. If you fancy a visit to the shops, you'll enjoy it more if you can take someone along to keep you company. They'll also be able to tell you whether all those clothes you want to try on suit you.

• *Tuesday 5 March* •

There's quite a nip in the air today but it's got nothing to do with the weather. It's coming from the direction of a loved one or authority figure, and you may feel powerless to do much about it. It's highly likely that you think this person disapproves of you for some reason. Maybe they've ticked you off or they seem to be looking down their nose at you? Try not to take this too much to heart – you may even have forgotten all about it in a couple of days' time.

• *Wednesday 6 March* •

Tempers flare today and you'll probably come in for your fair share of the flak at some point. But do you really think you're getting your fair share or are you getting more of it than you deserve? From your standpoint, someone is being overemotional and dredging up the past. Their sense of grievance may even make them dwell on imagined slights and slurs. Unfortunately it will be horribly easy to fall into this trap yourself. By all means stick up for yourself if necessary but don't imagine that the whole world is out to get you.

• *Thursday 7 March* •

After the past couple of days, it's hardly surprising that your emotions are still near the surface. It won't take much to make you feel upset or jangled today, especially if there are problems in dealing with a woman. You may suspect that she's feeling jealous or envious of you, or perhaps she's going out of her way to be difficult. Try to let her get on with it and don't become involved. She can make someone else's life a misery for a change!

• *Friday 8 March* •

You've had a basinful of problems during the past few days and you've now reached breaking point. If you're absolutely fed up with the way a certain someone is behaving, this is your chance to put your foot down. But be careful how you do this because you may sound more forceful than you intended. If you come on too strong or insist on having everything your way, you'll encounter a lot of opposition and bad feeling. So take it gently.

• *Saturday 9 March* •

You need some light relief! It's been a tough week but you're now ready to put the whole thing behind you and relax. If possible, do something that you've never tried before or visit somewhere for the first time. This is also a great day to think about the future. You might decide to arrange a holiday so you've got something to look forward to, or how about working hard on your plans for the future? You'll want to give them your best shot now.

• *Sunday 10 March* •

Try not to do too many things at once today. You don't want to hang around twiddling your thumbs but being in too much of a hurry could lead to annoying mistakes and possibly even a minor mishap. Be very careful when handling hot or sharp objects, especially if you're thinking about something else at the time. Work off any pent-up energy at the gym or by going for a brisk walk. Otherwise the fur will fly!

• *Monday 11 March* •

If you're wondering why your relationships have been so tricky recently, start talking to the people concerned. Between now and late March is the ideal opportunity to talk about what happened, thrash out your differences and then call a truce. It's also a great time to get involved in discussions and negotiations because you'll enjoy having your say, but you'll want everyone else to get a chance to speak as well.

• *Tuesday 12 March* •

Money burns a massive hole in your pockets today, so beware if you're already trying to stretch your budget like a piece of elastic. It's one of those days when you simply can't resist temptation because you want to enjoy yourself as much as possible. If you've had your eye on someone who's only been a friend until now, things could develop between you in quite a steamy and sultry way. It looks as though the platonic stage of your relationship has been consigned to the past!

• *Wednesday 13 March* •

A certain someone is in danger of letting their feelings run away with them today. Try to make sure that you don't behave like this too! It's a great day for clearing the air with someone by getting everything out into the open, but keep a grip on yourself and don't turn minor problems into massive melodramas. It may also be tempting to dredge up old scores or to brood on the way someone treated you in the past, but that will only make you feel more miserable.

• *Thursday 14 March* •

Team work is very important right now, even though it isn't going quite as easily as you'd like. Nevertheless, the coming fortnight is a very auspicious time to join forces with other people. You'll have much more success if you can work as part of a team than if you're toiling away by yourself, even if it's only a temporary alliance. It's also a marvellous opportunity to reach an agreement with someone and know that it will stand the test of time.

• *Friday 15 March* •

Someone is really good company today. They're funny, generous and full of good ideas. In fact, it does you good just to be near them. It's a super day for simply enjoying yourself, but it's also great if you want to ask someone a favour or get on the right side of them. Something else that will work out well is to think about your plans for the future – you'll come up with inspired, big ideas.

• *Saturday 16 March* •

You're in a very understanding and compassionate mood today. You're prepared to make allowances for people and also to give them the benefit of the doubt. That's great if you want to put the recent kerfuffles behind you, without assigning any blame about who did what. If you know someone who's under the weather or going through a bad time at the moment, think about what you can do to make their life a little easier.

• *Sunday 17 March* •

Your thoughts take a serious turn today. They may even be tinged with gloominess or pessimism, because it's highly likely that you're seeing things in the worst possible light. For instance, if you have a disagreement with someone or there's a coolness between you, you'll tell yourself that this is the start of a major rift between you when it may only be a temporary blip. If you ask someone for advice, you may not get a very cheery or positive answer, so be warned.

• *Monday 18 March* •

Almost nothing can stop you achieving what you set out to do today! You have an indefatigable desire to make things happen, and everyone else can only sit back in wonder as you get things done. This is an especially good day for doing something that requires courage or bravado because you have plenty of both right now. Any activities that strive to make the world a better place get your vote now and you'll try to persuade others to lend a hand.

• *Tuesday 19 March* •

Everyone is wonderfully easy to get on with today, which makes a nice change from recent events! Make the most of it while it lasts! It's a terrific day to be with people who are on the same wavelength as you and you'll enjoy swapping ideas with each other. This is also a good opportunity to get together with people from other cultures and countries. You'll learn a lot from one another, including the fact that any obvious differences don't matter.

• *Wednesday 20 March* •

If you want to stand up for yourself or defend your ideas, you'll have no problems at all today. Your words and ideas will flow, and you'll be able to get your point across without making a big song and dance about it. If your thoughts keep straying to holidays and long-distance travel, you could be tempted to book up a trip on the spur of the moment. Or maybe someone is trying to talk you into it? If so, you won't have to think twice!

• *Thursday 21 March* •

Intense emotions threaten to overwhelm you today. Someone could easily penetrate your defences and get under your skin, so you get into a right old state. That's especially likely if this person thinks they have an emotional or moral hold over you. If you want to clear the air with someone, this is a good day to do it provided you're ready for the emotional fallout that's bound to follow.

• *Friday 22 March* •

This is another day when you're poised on the brink of staging a scene. If someone disagrees with you or tries to talk you into doing something against your will, you'll resist them with as much energy as you can muster. This could soon turn into a stalemate between the two of you. Watch out for signs of obsessive thinking, when something goes round and round inside your head to the exclusion of all else. It will waste an awful lot of time and energy!

• *Saturday 23 March* •

Relax and enjoy yourself! Even if you've got a hectic schedule today, try to set aside some time when you can have some fun and forget all about the chores. Friends are especially good company now because they'll take you out of yourself. Any form of group activity is also looking good, as it will give you the chance to get together with people on the same wavelength as you. Don't be surprised if you have to act as a leader or you're expected to set an example.

• *Sunday 24 March* •

Give someone a hug! You're feeling far more emotional and demonstrative than usual so it would be a shame to let the day go by without letting someone know how much you care about them. It's unlikely that you'll want to do this under everyone's noses because you're much more interested in retaining your privacy. So why not take this person by the hand and disappear into the sunset together? If you've been plucking up the courage to declare your feelings, there'll be no stopping you now!

• *Monday 25 March* •

Try to think before you speak today. Otherwise, you'll open your mouth and put your foot straight in it! Yes, it's one of those days when you're outspoken and have a tendency to drop clangers. This is even more likely if you're feeling het up or someone has offended you. Alternatively, you'll have to deal with someone else who's suffering from foot in mouth disease. They're digging a pit for themselves but they don't realize it!

• *Tuesday 26 March* •

Don't be too hard on yourself today. You're looking at life from a rather gloomy perspective and you'll quickly zero in on any faults that you perceive in yourself and then give yourself a hard time over them. Once you start to do this, you'll feel miserable and depressed in no time at all. You may also have problems because duties and responsibilities are weighing heavily on your shoulders. But are things really as bad as they seem?

• *Wednesday 27 March* •

Keep a close eye on your finances today otherwise they could run away with you. You're even more likely to spend money if you're with a friend because they'll talk you into all sorts of extravagances. These seem like a good idea at the time but they could work out expensive. Despite this, friends are great to have around now. One chum in particular may bring an opportunity your way or help you to turn a dream into reality.

• *Thursday 28 March* •

If you went overboard financially yesterday, today's Full Moon is a timely reminder that you may need to sort things out. Perhaps you need to make some economies or work out a strict budget that you can stick to? The coming fortnight is also a good opportunity to consider whether you place too much importance on your possessions and status symbols. You may decide that other areas of your life have more value.

• *Friday 29 March* •

The financial mood continues today and you're now ready to turn your penetrating gaze on all joint and official money matters. This phase will last until mid-April so you have plenty of time to unravel any problems. It's also a good chance to think about your close relationships and whether they give you what you want. If things aren't going very well, perhaps you should talk things through. It may also help to think about whether you're repeating a pattern from other relationships and whether you're happy to let this continue.

• *Saturday 30 March* •

If you want to add a sparkle to your day, do something different from your usual Saturday routine. A change of scene will do you the world of good, as will doing something for the first time. There might also be a little flirtation in the air, when you're very attracted to a certain someone. Are you going to leave it at that or do you have high hopes of your relationship turning into something more serious and long-lasting?

• *Sunday 31 March* •

Listen carefully and you'll benefit from someone's wisdom and experience. This could happen when you ask them for their advice or it may be the by-product of a conversation with them. It's certainly a good day to be with people who are older or wiser than you. If you're at work, you'll get on well with people in authority. You may also get the chance to show how good you are at your job, and in time that could lead to promotion or added responsibilities.

APRIL AT A GLANCE

Love	♥ ♥ ♥ ♥
Money	£ $ £ $ £
Career	💻 💻 💻 💻
Health	☼ ☼

• *Monday 1 April* •

Fresh horizons are beckoning! You're starting to think about your next holiday and any other excuse to go travelling as well. During the next three weeks there could also be a romantic encounter with someone who comes from another walk of life. Your many differences will bring you together rather than drive you apart. It all adds up to plenty to look forward to, and that isn't an April fool joke!

• *Tuesday 2 April* •

Think big! You've got some great ideas floating around in your mind so don't let them go to waste. You're especially inspired when it comes to thinking about your plans for the future and considering your current financial situation. You might make some leaps of the imagination that turn out to be sheer brilliance, so don't place any restrictions on your thoughts.

• *Wednesday 3 April* •

What a wonderful day! You're in a very happy and relaxed mood, so enjoy it while it lasts. The ideal way to spend the day is with some of your favourite people because you'll want to make a big fuss of them – and they'll want to do the same to you. If you've been having problems with a loved one recently, this is the perfect chance to charm yourself back into their good books. You might also enjoy spending money but it might be rather expensive because you can't resist temptation.

• *Thursday 4 April* •

You had some wild flights of the imagination on Tuesday and your mind is working well again today. But this time you're in a much more sober, pragmatic and constructive sort of mood. You aren't prepared to waste time thinking about or working on projects that you know will never see the light of day. You only want to deal with reality, so forget about wishful thinking or if-onlys and concentrate on the facts.

• *Friday 5 April* •

Life is looking pretty good! You're feeling full of energy and you want to get as much out of the day as possible. It's fantastic for doing something enjoyable but active – how about being sporty or athletic? You're also feeling competitive but aren't placing too much importance on winning, so it's great for pitting your skills against those of other people. If you're with children, they'll run you off your feet but be good fun at the same time.

• *Saturday 6 April* •

Feelings run high today, especially if someone isn't very well or has got over-tired. Even someone who's usually calm and contented could get in a bit of a state now, although it won't last long. You may also have to deal with a woman who is being rather tricky or who feels envious of someone else's good fortune. But it isn't all bad by any means. If you're at work, it's a good chance to get closer to one of your colleagues or customers.

• *Sunday 7 April* •

You're able to do a lot of deep thinking today. You can look at a subject in a very clear manner so you can get right to the heart of it without being sidetracked by superficial ideas. What's more, whatever you say will be very honest and straightforward, so everyone can count on you to tell them the facts instead of what you think they want to hear. While you're about it, you'll be able to clear up any muddles connected with your home or official finances.

• *Monday 8 April* •

You're raring to go and there's certainly a lot you want to achieve today. But be careful how you go about it. You may be in such a hurry to accomplish something that you're prepared to cut corners, and that could lead to problems later on. Also, you might easily get in a bit of a state and feel irritated with people if you think they aren't pulling their weight or working as fast as you'd like. Take a deep breath and take things more slowly!

• *Tuesday 9 April* •

If you're a typical Virgo you aren't usually idealistic but today you're not viewing things in their true light. Perhaps your emotions have got in the way and you're feeling very subjective about someone or something? You may also have to deal with someone who is behaving like a saint and a martyr rolled into one, but who is really neither of those things and instead is on a massive ego trip about how wonderful they are.

• *Wednesday 10 April* •

Any hint of restrictions or limitations will have you fuming today. You're simply not prepared to be tied down or told what you can and can't do. Be very careful if you're at work because you won't take kindly to people issuing orders or telling you what to do. It's certainly not a good day to ask for some time off or to take a long lunch hour if it's a busy period because that will annoy everyone else and could result in an argument.

• *Thursday 11 April* •

You're in a marvellously organized mood today. It's great for sorting out anything that's been bothering you recently. Financial matters are grist to your mill now and you'll soon get to grips with paperwork, figures or complex facts. You may even end up advising other people who are struggling to understand business or contractual details. You're a very impressive proposition right now and a boss or authority figure will be very taken with you.

• *Friday 12 April* •

Today's New Moon is giving you a big hint. Over the next two weeks, pay careful attention to the financial provisions you've made for your future, such as pensions and insurance policies. If you haven't yet arranged a pension, for instance, this is a good chance to get some expert advice on whether you need one. Or maybe you'd rather start a long-term savings scheme that will eventually give you a nice nest egg?

• *Saturday 13 April* •

Between now and the end of April your mind will be buzzing with excitement. It's going to be a phase when you're full of curiosity about the world and you aren't content with your current level of knowledge. You want to know more about all sorts of interesting subjects. You might decide to enrol for a formal course of education or it could happen in ways you don't really notice at the time, such as reading the newspaper from cover to cover, paying more attention to the news bulletins or talking to someone about their experiences. Keep an open mind and you'll learn a lot.

• *Sunday 14 April* •

You're starting to feel fired with ambition and this flame will burn within you until late May. During this time you won't want to sit around doing nothing. Instead, you'll have a real urge to achieve something that you can be proud of and which other people will respect. It's a marvellous opportunity to apply for promotion, for instance. If you're self-employed, it's a good chance to make new contacts or put in for a job that will bring you lots of kudos and money. You're capable of achieving a lot right now.

• *Monday 15 April* •

You're determined to start as you mean to go on, so it's a great day for getting an ambition one stage nearer to reality. You don't want anything or anyone to hold you back, and woe betide them if they do because they'll get a piece of your mind! This is something you need to watch for because you aren't as flexible as usual and you could easily bite off someone's head if they say or do things that you don't agree with.

• *Tuesday 16 April* •

If you stepped out of line yesterday, don't be surprised if you have to face the music today. You might get a big finger-wagging from someone who takes a dim view of your actions, and they'll expect you to be penitent. Try to pace yourself at work otherwise you may take on too much and then feel utterly exhausted by it. Even so, you may feel duty bound to shoulder a responsibility that weighs heavily on you.

• *Wednesday 17 April* •

If you're stuck for ideas, listen carefully to other people's suggestions because they could come up with some crackers. This is a terrific day to enjoy using your brain, especially if you're busy with a favourite hobby or you're studying a subject that stretches your imagination and makes you think. If you suspect your social life could do with spicing up, consider joining a club or society that caters for one of your interests. It might be the start of an exciting new chapter in your life. Go on – you won't know until you try.

• *Thursday 18 April* •

This is a fantastic day to use your imagination and do some daydreaming. But it's a different story if you want to concentrate on facts or you're doing something very complex, because your brain simply won't play ball. It's one of those days when your mind drifts from one subject to another and it's hard to keep track of your thoughts. You may also have some very strange ways of seeing the world which won't go down too well with anyone expecting you to stick to the facts.

• *Friday 19 April* •

If you're worried that you made some silly mistakes yesterday, check what you've done just in case you made any howlers. After that, you'll enjoy talking to people who have an interesting take on life. For instance, chatting to someone who comes from another culture might provide you with some fascinating insights into what makes them tick. It's also a super day for treating yourself to a new book or browsing round the shelves in the local library.

• *Saturday 20 April* •

Your current thirst for adventure and knowledge goes up a notch today, and over the next four weeks you'll want to identify with people and ideas that are cultivated, erudite and intelligent. This isn't a time to be content with the status quo because you've got such a strong urge to break out from your current routine and do something different for a change. Travel plans are almost impossible to resist now, so if you haven't yet booked up your next holiday it won't be long before you're visiting the travel agent.

• *Sunday 21 April* •

It's horribly easy to speak out of turn today, especially if someone catches you on the raw or says things that upset you. Unfortunately it will be almost impossible to stop yourself saying the wrong thing at the wrong time. Alternatively, you may have to deal with someone who manages to put both feet in it. If you're on the receiving end of their clanger, try not to take offence if you know perfectly well that they didn't mean it and it was simply a slip of the tongue.

• *Monday 22 April* •

The more positive your attitude today, the better the day will go. As a result, you might be offered a marvellous opportunity or you could get involved in a situation that works out really well for you. There could also be a fortunate encounter with someone who comes from another country or culture. This person might turn out to be a very lucky contact for you or they may simply be terrific fun and always good for a laugh.

• *Tuesday 23 April* •

What's bugging you? You're feeling het up and agitated, and it won't take much to make you completely blow your top. It's very tempting to take out your bad mood on whoever happens to be around, but it won't be fair to get angry with people who are merely innocent bystanders. If you can't tick off the person who's annoyed you, perhaps because they're your boss and you don't want to lose your job, work off steam by doing something physical, otherwise your frustrated anger will ruin the day.

• *Wednesday 24 April* •

There are some surprises at work today, so stand by! You might get a last-minute chance to try something for the first time. Or you might suddenly realize that a colleague is really attractive, even if you've never spotted their charms before. If you are attracted to someone they probably aren't your usual type and you'll be mystified about why they're making you go weak at the knees.

• *Thursday 25 April* •

Want to butter up a boss or convince a superior that you're the person for the job? Then launch a charm offensive between now and mid-May, and see what happens. During this time you might also be completely smitten by someone who is richer, older or more influential than you. If this happens, be honest with yourself about the real reasons for the big attraction. Is it because of the power this person wields, or do you want to bask in their reflected glory? Or is there another reason?

• *Friday 26 April* •

Keep a firm hand on your wallet or purse today if you're trying to control your spending. Otherwise those notes and coins will be flying in all directions before you can say 'I'll take it'. Yes, it's one of those days when you're tempted to splash out on all sorts of irresistible items. That's fine if you can afford it but it's not such good news if you're wondering how to stretch your finances until the next pay day.

• *Saturday 27 April* •

Questions about a child's education or a neighbour's behaviour come to the fore over the next two weeks, and you'll have to do some serious thinking. Don't expect the answer to appear in your mind like magic – it may be more elusive than that. The coming fortnight is also a good chance to sort out any problems or muddles that have sprung up with a certain person. A few well-chosen words could make all the difference to your relationship and restore the peace once more.

• *Sunday 28 April* •

Keep calm! It's surprisingly easy to get rattled and upset today, especially if you're seeing some of the family or doing some entertaining. You might be worried about what you're cooking or you may have to be nice to a woman who's being tiresome or demanding. Family problems might also threaten to disturb your equilibrium, especially if they stir up difficult memories or put you on the defensive. Count to ten and try to keep your cool.

• *Monday 29 April* •

By the time you rest your head on the pillow tonight you should be feeling really pleased with yourself! You'll achieve a lot today, and without going at it hammer and tongs. In fact, steady progress will be much more satisfying and productive than trying to do fifty things at once. You will also benefit from the help and co-operation of workmates and people in authority, and you'll feel good to know that you've got their backing.

• *Tuesday 30 April* •

It's time to think carefully about your job prospects. Are they everything you could possibly want or would they benefit from some help? If you want to improve your current situation, consider adding another string to your bow. Is there a new qualification that will boost your earning power or a skill that needs brushing up? If you're toying with the idea of a completely new career, start finding out about how and where to retrain.

MAY AT A GLANCE

Love	♥ ♥
Money	£
Career	💻 💻 💻 💻 💻
Health	☼ ☼

• *Wednesday 1 May* •

You're feeling really positive and optimistic today, and with good reason. Even if life has been tough recently, you feel much better about it suddenly and are convinced that your glass is half full rather than half empty. This is a very attractive attitude as far as other people are concerned and they'll enjoy your company because you're feeling so jolly. You might even make a new friend as a result of your cheerful mood.

• *Thursday 2 May* •

Your social life doesn't go entirely according to plan today. If you've arranged to meet up with someone it might be a good idea to doublecheck the time and venue with them before you set off. Otherwise, you may be hanging around in one place while your chum is waiting for you somewhere completely different. If you were sure that you-know-who was going to ask you out today or do anything else that you've been longing for, you could be disappointed. But don't worry – this frustrating phase won't last long.

• *Friday 3 May* •

Things go really well at work today. It's an especially good day for taking part in a meeting, interview or discussion because you'll have no qualms about putting forward your ideas or standing up for what you believe in. It's also a super day for getting your point across in ways that everyone can understand and which make you seem very articulate and intelligent. Which you are, of course!

• *Saturday 4 May* •

Provided you can focus your energies and concentrate on your topmost priorities, today will go very well. You'll be pleased with the progress you make and other people will be very impressed by your prowess. It's great for working on a project that will boost your reputation or your job prospects. But it won't be such a successful day if you fritter away your energy or try to do too many things at once.

• *Sunday 5 May* •

Do yourself a favour and have a break from your usual Sunday routine. If you don't, you'll soon start to feel bored, restless and irritable, and that will lead to a very difficult day all round. Ideally, you should do something that you've never tried before, even if it's as modest as visiting a new shop, experimenting with some unusual food ingredients or going to a restaurant that's only just opened.

• *Monday 6 May* •

Pace yourself today or you'll end up with very little to show for all your efforts. You'll be so wrapped up in doing things quickly that you'll end up in a muddle or having to do everything twice. Keep a tight rein on your temper when talking to people in authority or power. Otherwise you might say something in the heat of the moment that comes back to haunt you when you've simmered down.

• *Tuesday 7 May* •

Look after yourself today. You're going through a very industrious phase at the moment and it's very satisfying, but this is one of those days when you might go over the top and try to do too much. As a result, you'll feel over-emotional and possibly even tearful. You may also imagine that certain people are being distant and reserved with you, almost as though they've gone off you or they disapprove of something you've done. Be careful not to read too much into tricky situations.

• *Wednesday 8 May* •

Whatever you do today, don't force anyone into doing things against their will. Even what seems like a little gentle persuasion on your part may feel like excessive coercion to the other person, and they'll come down on you like a ton of bricks or dig their heels in and refuse to budge. This is especially likely if you're trying to talk a loved one into seeing things from your point of view. They have their own ideas right now and it may be a waste of breath trying to make them change their mind.

• *Thursday 9 May* •

If you couldn't change someone's mind yesterday you won't have any better luck today. It certainly isn't a good idea to use emotional blackmail in an effort to get them to play ball. In fact, it will prejudice your case and cause a lot of bad feeling. If you're on the receiving end of someone's not so subtle persuasion, you'll feel as though you're being browbeaten by some unfair tactics. Don't be shy about standing up to this person.

• *Friday 10 May* •

All the tension of the past few days comes to a head today, resulting in a massive row or showdown. It's very important to get your feelings out into the open but try not to go over the top if it isn't really necessary. On a lighter note, there could be a tremendous flirtation between you and someone you meet through work. The question is whether this is the start of something big or just a bit of light-hearted fun. You may not know the answer yet!

• *Saturday 11 May* •

What have you got planned this weekend? If you're at a bit of a loose end, how about taking off on a last-minute break? You'll really enjoy having a change of scene, especially if you can combine it with a visit to friends that you haven't seen in a while. You'll also enjoy activities connected to a favourite hobby or pastime, and they'll be a delightful antidote to the stresses of the past few days.

• *Sunday 12 May* •

How do you feel about the prospect of lots of super opportunities coming your way over the next two weeks? Are you excited? That's good, because then you'll have a ball over the coming fortnight! To get the most out of this marvellous phase, be as open-minded and receptive to new ideas as possible. Don't discount anything until you know all the facts, especially if you're faced by something or someone that's an unknown quantity. They might turn out to be exactly what you've been waiting for!

• *Monday 13 May* •

If you want to concentrate on details or do something fiddly, this is the day to roll up your sleeves and get on with it. Your powers of concentration are good and you've got the patience to work hard at something until you get it right. Even so, make sure you get plenty of breaks otherwise you'll end up feeling stale, and you may also find it hard to see the wood for the trees.

• *Tuesday 14 May* •

Play your cards right and you'll be able to spin a huge web of charm around a certain person today. So if you want to impress a boss or get on the right side of someone in authority, this is the day to do it. They'll find it hard to resist you, provided you don't overdo the sugary sweetness and make them wonder if you've got an ulterior motive. If that happens, they may be very suspicious of you.

• *Wednesday 15 May* •

Communications in business and your career start to go slightly pear-shaped from today and they won't straighten themselves out again until early June. During this period you should try to avoid making legal or binding commitments in case you change your mind about them or you discover later on that they aren't worth the paper they're written on. If you have no choice but to sign on the dotted line before early June, make sure you read the small print very carefully indeed.

• *Thursday 16 May* •

A friend is a real chum today. They'll make you laugh and take you out of yourself. They may also do you a favour without even being asked, or maybe the boot's on the other foot and you're the one who steps into the breach at the first hint of trouble. If you're out and about today you might even meet someone who promises to be a new chum. If so, don't be shy about chatting to them or asking if you can meet up in the future.

• *Friday 17 May* •

You've got a spring in your step today. You feel great! Things are looking up and you've got plenty to smile about. Even if your schedule is crammed with work commitments, try to fit in something that you can look forward to and which will help you to relax. A drink with a friend might be just what you need, or maybe you fancy a trip to your favourite bookshop so you can buy something new to read.

• *Saturday 18 May* •

If you're the sort of Virgo who is usually embarrassed to acknowledge your true feelings, even to yourself, this will be a very useful day. You'll find it much easier than usual to know how you feel about things and you can let your emotions flow. Memories may occupy a large part of your thoughts but don't block them because they could give you valuable clues about the current state of your emotions.

• *Sunday 19 May* •

Go carefully today and try not to restrict yourself in any way. Any hint that you're being limited or hampered will make you want to rebel and claim your independence, probably in rather dramatic or difficult ways. If you want to kick up some dust and shock everyone around you, this is definitely the day to do it! Perhaps you need to vary your routine in some creative and imaginative ways, so you've got more personal freedom and more scope to do what you want?

• *Monday 20 May* •

Get out your glad rags because you're going to be in great demand during the next few weeks! Your social life is about to take off and friends will want to be with you as much as possible. As well as meeting up your current friends, it's a marvellous opportunity to pick up the threads with chums that you haven't seen in a while. Have a look through your address book and get in touch with the people who you rarely see from one year's end to the next.

• *Tuesday 21 May* •

If you've been working hard recently, all that effort is about to get its reward. You might find yourself in the limelight during the next few weeks or there could be the prospect of promotion at long last. If you're considering looking for a better job, get on the trail now and things could go your way. Don't be shy about asking an expert for their advice, perhaps by signing up with a specialist employment agency or asking someone to look over your CV and suggest ways to improve it.

• *Wednesday 22 May* •

If you're at work today you'll find it really easy to get on well with everyone you meet. Even the people who are usually a complete pain in the neck seem to have mellowed temporarily, making them much more pleasant to deal with than usual. Make the most of this amenable atmosphere while it lasts! If you're involved in a business meeting or job interview today, everyone will be very impressed by what you say and do.

• *Thursday 23 May* •

You're full of enthusiasm and energy today, especially when it comes to your work. This is a marvellous time to concentrate on your career and long-term plans because you're so committed to making them a success. Today, you're prepared to work away at whatever needs to be done, and you've even got enough will power to tackle those jobs that you don't enjoy or which are a bit of a chore. They won't seem nearly as bad as usual.

• *Friday 24 May* •

How are your finances shaping up? This is a good opportunity to keep an eye on them and make sure everything is ticking over nicely. It's also a marvellous chance to buy something that will boost your ego or enhance your appearance. If you're looking for a new outfit for work, take a look round the shops today because you might spot the very thing you need. Look for items that are classic and won't date, and preferably that are made from natural fabrics.

• *Saturday 25 May* •

Ready to have some fun? Try to put work to one side today and concentrate on enjoyment instead. You'll feel great if you can get out of the house and visit somewhere that always lifts your spirits. And if you can do it in the company of a lively friend or close relative, so much the better! Neighbourhood activities are good fun as well now and could lead to you making some new contacts.

• *Sunday 26 May* •

Take a look around your home or office today. Is it cluttered with things that you no longer need? If so, this is a fantastic opportunity to grab some bin bags and start chucking away all those things that are simply gathering dust. You might also decide to do this on a psychological level, by letting go of memories that make you unhappy or angry. This won't happen overnight but it's the perfect day to set the process in motion. During the months ahead you'll really start to feel the benefits.

• *Monday 27 May* •

You've been working really hard recently and you're pleased with your progress, but your single-minded devotion may not be going down very well in certain quarters. If members of the family are complaining that they never see you or you're always too tired to do anything other than flop on the sofa every night, it's time to see if you can find a balance between professional and domestic demands. At the very least, discuss what's wrong and let everyone know the reasons for your current unavailability.

• *Tuesday 28 May* •

You know what they say about all work and no play, and you're starting to long for some light relief. During the next few weeks you'll become increasingly interested in your hobbies and pastimes. You might even decide that you want to turn one of them into some pin money or eventually make it your full-time career. If the thought of this really appeals to you, start exploring your options so you know whether it's merely a pipe dream or a real possibility.

• *Wednesday 29 May* •

There's a lot going on today and you want to get involved in as much of it as possible! It's a shame you can't clone yourself because it's almost inevitable that you'll have to miss out on something. For instance, you might get two invitations for the same day and have to choose between them, or you may have to decide whether to spend time with a friend or loved one. But whatever decision you reach, you're determined that it won't spoil your fun!

• *Thursday 30 May* •

Speak up! This is a fantastic day for saying what you think, especially if you've got the ear of a superior or authority figure. They'll listen carefully to what you say. It's also a good chance to catch up with correspondence that's overdue or to fill in some forms. If you're still toying with the idea of learning a new skill or adding to your qualifications, find out more about what's involved.

• *Friday 31 May* •

You end the month on a high note, particularly where work is concerned. It seems that everyone is pleased with you and they're also easy to get along with right now. Long may it last! If you've been postponing getting in touch with someone because they're always so crusty or unpleasant to deal with, they're in a much better mood today and may even be almost human! Make contact with them before they revert to type once more.

JUNE AT A GLANCE

Love	♥ ♥
Money	£
Career	💻 💻 💻 💻 💻
Health	☼ ☼

• *Saturday 1 June* •

How are you feeling? This is a terrific day to take a little more care of your health than you've done recently, especially if you've been run ragged by the amount of work you've been doing. So why not postpone the chores to another day and pamper yourself for a change? You'll enjoy investigating a complementary therapy, having a relaxing massage or unwinding near a stretch of water. After all, you deserve it!

• *Sunday 2 June* •

It's a frustrating day because lots of trivial things are likely to go wrong. If you're getting very annoyed because of the current communication difficulties at work, it won't take much to make you lose your temper now. You may also get impatient with someone who you think is dragging their heels or not giving you the answers you need. But maybe their hands are tied, or they're as much in the dark as you are?

• *Monday 3 June* •

Once again your patience is stretched to the limit and it won't take much to make it snap completely. Something happens that will be the final straw, making you irritated and determined that someone should take the blame. Go carefully if you're at work because you won't be popular if you start creating havoc or yelling at people for no good reason. And even if you are justified in shouting at someone, you should try to moderate yourself and not go OTT.

• *Tuesday 4 June* •

Pay close attention to your official and joint finances today. Maybe you aren't getting a very good rate of interest on your savings and you should look for a better return on your money? Or maybe your current credit card isn't offering you all the perks you want? Start doing some research to see if you can find a better deal and don't be shy about asking your associates if they've got any recommendations.

• *Wednesday 5 June* •

Have you been neglecting a certain person lately because you've been so busy with other things? If so, make a massive fuss of them today so they know it's nothing personal. It will work wonders for your relationship and help to bring the two of you closer together. This is also a good day for discussing going into partnership with someone, whether it's for business or pleasure. Try to postpone making your decision until the 8th, when the picture is much clearer.

• *Thursday 6 June* •

You're in a very organized and practical mood today, making it a good chance to carry on sorting out your finances. You've got a great eye for detail now so there's no danger that you'll overlook anything important. If someone wants to confide in you, you'll listen carefully and try to give them good advice if they ask for it. But bear in mind that they may simply want to unburden themselves to you.

• *Friday 7 June* •

Something that you're involved in is about to hit crisis point. For instance, if you're trying to make big changes to your home or your working life, you may meet some powerful opposition to your plans. This won't be easy to cope with and it may even feel like a struggle for survival on an emotional level because you've got so much invested in it. The last thing you should do is to bulldoze your way through other people's objections and force them to agree with you because that will only make matters worse. Listen to them – maybe they have a point.

• *Saturday 8 June* •

Phew! From today you can start unravelling the communications problems you've been saddled with since the middle of May. You need to make up for lost time, especially if you've been delaying reaching important decisions or you've got a pile of paperwork that urgently needs your attention. Over the next few days you may also receive some official post that's been delayed or you may hear from someone important who's been unavailable recently.

• *Sunday 9 June* •

You're a very powerful proposition today! You know exactly what you want to achieve and you have the backbone and sheer grit to get it done. It's a wonderful day for impressing people with your abilities but be prepared to work hard in the process. Things aren't going to fall into your lap right now – they require a lot of effort but this will be worth it in the long run. There are only two provisos – don't work yourself into the ground and make sure you have faith in yourself.

• *Monday 10 June* •

Today's Eclipsed New Moon adds power to your elbow and reinforces the fact that you're sitting very pretty right now! Your career prospects and self-confidence receive a massive boost from today and you'll feel the effects for the rest of the month. If you're a typical Virgo you're very modest but this isn't the time to take a back seat and let other people steal your thunder. If there's something you want to achieve, go all out for it this June. You know you can do it!

• *Tuesday 11 June* •

You're feeling really energized and vibrant, and no wonder with such glittering prospects ahead of you! What's more, your enthusiasm is very infectious and other people want a share of it. You could come up with some great ideas today, especially if they're rather unusual, so don't ignore them. One of them could be a winner! You'll also think of ways to inject more spice into your daily routine.

• *Wednesday 12 June* •

Think about your plans for the future today. You're keen to get moving on them and you don't want to hang about while other people decide whether they want to be involved or not. This may make you rather impatient and you could easily lose your rag with someone who you think is holding out on you or wasting your time. Remind them that you're waiting for them to make up their mind and then leave it at that. You don't want to spoil things by yelling at them.

• *Thursday 13 June* •

If you think you overstepped the mark yesterday, you'll want to apologize today. And who could resist you, because you're in such a light-hearted and amenable mood! This is a lovely day to get together with friends. You'll enjoy being part of a group and you'll welcome the chance to let your hair down. If you're hoping to turn a hobby into a money-making exercise, there could be some good news.

• *Friday 14 June* •

Between now and early July your emotions will become quite complicated, and at times you may not even know how you feel about certain things. That may be because you don't want to admit the truth to yourself, or perhaps it's because things are still evolving and you haven't yet made up your mind about them. Romance may be in the air as well, and you might even get involved in a relationship that has to be completely hush-hush. Sounds intriguing!

• *Saturday 15 June* •

Try to spend today catching your breath and relaxing whenever you get the chance. You've been working really hard lately and you need a rest! It's also a great day for being with people who you respect and admire, especially if you want to tell them about everything you've been doing recently. You might even want to pick their brains or benefit from their experience.

• *Sunday 16 June* •

If you've been keeping something under wraps recently, this is a marvellous chance to talk about it. Of course, you may want to be selective about who you confide in, but once you've done that you'll welcome the opportunity to talk. If you're involved in a charitable or voluntary activity you may be faced with a lot of paperwork or phone calls today, yet you'll be happy to do what you can to help.

• *Monday 17 June* •

Whoops! Someone's got the bit between their teeth today and they're determined not to let go. This person has very set ideas about things and they don't expect anyone to disagree with them. If you stand up to them, you'll know all about it. Yet you're not prepared to be steamrollered into submission by this person, nor do you want them to think they can always get their own way by behaving badly or acting like a petty tyrant.

• *Tuesday 18 June* •

Today looks like being a repeat performance of yesterday's ructions. If you stood your ground yesterday, you'll have to do it all over again today. But by now you aren't prepared to mince your words, so woe betide the person on the end of your tirade! Even though you're angry, make sure you direct your ire at the person who caused it – don't use the scattergun approach in which everyone gets the flak whether they deserve it or not.

• *Wednesday 19 June* •

The atmosphere returns to normal today, thank goodness. Put the whole thing behind you and concentrate on matters that you feel are important, either materially or emotionally. If you never seem to have the time for whatever or whoever makes your world go round, think carefully about how you can redress the balance. Someone older or wiser may be able to help you with this, so don't be shy about asking their advice.

• *Thursday 20 June* •

You have a strong appreciation for beauty today. If you work in a creative or artistic field you'll really enjoy yourself, and you'll love designing or making something that's attractive. If your work centres on other things, how about visiting an art gallery or museum in your lunch hour? Or maybe you'd prefer to relax in a favourite park or stretch of countryside? If you've got the day off, you'll want to spend it in some beautiful surroundings.

• *Friday 21 June* •

Friends play an important role in your life from today, and over the next four weeks you'll get a big kick out of being with your chums. If you've recently moved to a new area and you've left your friends behind, or there are other reasons for being short on pals, use this time as a chance to build up a new social circle. One of the easiest ways to do this is to join a club or group that caters for one of your interests, so you've already got something in common with everyone you meet.

• *Saturday 22 June* •

Keep cool! You're very impatient, jittery and edgy today, and the more cooped up and restricted you feel, the worse it will get. The only answer is to abandon your usual Saturday routine whenever possible and do something radically different instead. If you don't manage to do this you'll feel cheated and agitated, as though something is missing. It will also help to keep on the move. But don't be surprised if you have a surprise visitor or things don't go quite according to plan.

• *Sunday 23 June* •

The higher you've put someone on a pedestal, the more disappointed you'll feel now when the scales fall from your eyes and you realize that they're a mere mortal after all. Try to be realistic about other people's failings, otherwise you may feel that they've let you down badly or they should be ashamed of themselves. If you have a very high opinion of yourself, or you don't allow yourself any lapses, you may also be disappointed in the way you handle things now. But maybe you've been expecting too much from yourself?

• *Monday 24 June* •

If a new colleague has joined the team at work, take them under your wing today. Get chatting to them and find out if they've got any problems that you can help them with. They'll be very grateful that you've taken the time for them. Health problems also benefit from today's influence. If your doctor hasn't managed to cure an ailment, maybe it's time to try a complementary therapy or to use the power of thought to make it go away?

• *Tuesday 25 June* •

Enjoy being with your loved ones today. You'll feel a tremendous rapport with them and will really appreciate their company. You don't even have to do anything very special to feel happy. Sharing a bottle of wine with someone special, or curling up on the sofa with them in front of the TV, may be all you need to feel a warm glow of contentment. It's the little pleasures that mean the most now.

• *Wednesday 26 June* •

Someone charges through your life like a bull in a china shop today. They're feeling very unrestrained and they don't seem to care what they do or say. After only a few minutes of their company you'll feel as though you're in the path of a whirlwind. Perhaps the answer is to get out of their way until they've calmed down a bit! Otherwise you'll end up feeling exhausted and also rather frazzled from their high energy and the way they demand all your attention.

• *Thursday 27 June* •

Relax! This is the perfect day to stop whatever you're doing and take life easy for a change. You may even welcome the chance to down tools, especially if you're struggling to find the energy to do very much. Try to keep out of the way of anyone who's an obvious germ factory because you'll be very susceptible to catching their bugs. You should also avoid any food or drink that sometimes disagrees with you because it definitely won't do you any favours today.

• *Friday 28 June* •

A certain someone has very strong ideas today and they seem determined to ram them down your throat. Or are you the one who's doing all the talking and insisting that everyone listens to you? Either way, you can expect the fur to fly. If you want to talk people into seeing things from your point of view, this isn't the day to do it unless you're prepared to consider their opinions and let them have their say. If you aren't willing to meet people halfway, you'll have a real battle on your hands.

• *Saturday 29 June* •

After yesterday's dust-up, it's remarkably easy to get on well with everyone today. If you're going to a social event, expect to be surrounded by people who want to talk to you. You may even end up being the life and soul of the party! It's a super day for meeting someone for the first time because they could turn out to be a really good friend or possibly even a partner. If you're wondering which one, you'll just have to wait and see!

• *Sunday 30 June* •

It's the easiest thing in the world to speak out of turn now, but you'll kick yourself when you do. This is one of those days when your mouth seems to be working faster than your brain, and so you'll blurt out things that make you wince when you hear them. But it seems that other people are equally impatient and someone may try to hurry you into making a decision. If you aren't ready to make up your mind, don't let them browbeat you into saying yes or no.

JULY AT A GLANCE

Love	♥ ♥ ♥
Money	£ $
Career	💻 💻 💻 💻
Health	☼ ☼

• Monday 1 July •

Are you feeling a little down? It's more than likely at some point today because you're easily affected by other people. You may suspect that someone has a low opinion of you and worry how you can raise their estimation of you. Or you may feel duty bound to volunteer to do some overtime even though you don't want to. Try to deal with the facts and don't allow your imagination to conjure up all sorts of demons.

• Tuesday 2 July •

Concentrate! It's a marvellous day to focus on whatever needs to be done, especially at work. You'll find it easy to stick to the facts and it will be very satisfying to get so much work under your belt. If you're taking part in a negotiation or business meeting, everyone will be very impressed by the way you marshal your thoughts and say exactly what you mean. All the same, make sure you don't take on more than your fair share of work unless it's absolutely necessary, otherwise you'll become everyone's dogsbody.

• Wednesday 3 July •

You've got plenty of energy to burn up today, so what do you plan to do with it? Get out and about with some friends, especially if you're visiting somewhere that's adventurous or daring. Why not take that literally and visit an adventure park? If you can't spare the time, how about making some big plans for the future? You'll come up with some great ideas even though they'll be quite a challenge.

• *Thursday 4 July* •

You'll start to feel restless if you're cooped up in one place for too long today. What you need to do is inject an element of excitement into your routine, so try to do something that's a radical departure from your usual Thursday schedule. The people you mix with now might also keep things interesting, perhaps when they behave in ways you weren't expecting or you see a new side to their character. Don't take anyone for granted right now!

• *Friday 5 July* •

You're in a terrific mood! It's a lovely way to end the week because you're determined to have a good time. Ideally, you should get the hard work out of the way as soon as possible and concentrate on fun. Friends are wonderful company now and they'll open your eyes to all sorts of fresh opportunities and ideas. A favourite hobby or pastime is another great way to relax now and you'll want to put as much into it as possible.

• *Saturday 6 July* •

If you've been grappling with a work-related problem recently, try approaching it from a new angle today. Suddenly, light may dawn and you'll find the answer to your prayers. You certainly won't get anywhere if you continue to look at the problem in the same way you've done up to now. You may also have a flash of inspiration about a health matter or the way to deal with someone in authority over you.

• *Sunday 7 July* •

Thoughts about your future plans occupy your mind over the next two weeks. It's a great chance to think carefully about what you want to achieve during the rest of 2002 and beyond. Maybe there's something that you've always wanted to do but have never got around to before? If so, this might be the perfect opportunity to start it. Intellectual and humanitarian pursuits will also capture your interest now.

• *Monday 8 July* •

Watch out for someone who's behaving with all the subtlety of a Scud missile. They seem to have a bee in their bonnet about something and they're obviously reluctant to let the subject drop. They may also be keen to persuade you to behave in the way they want, and if you refuse to play ball they'll step up the emotional pressure and do their best to make you feel guilty. Remember, the only person who can control your feelings right now is you! Don't let this person dictate your reactions.

• *Tuesday 9 July* •

There are lots of surprises in store today, so be prepared for even the best-laid plans to go awry. You might discover a new side to someone and you may not be very pleased by what you see. If you're at work, a colleague may act in ways that leave you open-mouthed with astonishment. Be very careful of anyone who seems to be taking advantage of your good nature or who is manipulating a situation for their own ends.

• *Wednesday 10 July* •

Life has been slightly tough over the past few days but some light relief arrives today and it will remain until early August. During this time you'll enjoy a massive surge in your popularity, so expect to be deluged with invitations and to hear from lots of people who want to know how you are. Love might also brighten up your life, either when an existing relationship goes through a very happy phase or when you embark on a new affair. Either way, it sounds good!

• *Thursday 11 July* •

A friend is a real live wire today. There's no danger of things being boring while this person is around! If anything, life could get a little too hectic, especially if your friend is the sort of person who leaps into situations without thinking them through first. Before you know what's happened, they may have dragged you into their latest escapade. Never mind – it will be a lot of fun while it lasts.

• *Friday 12 July* •

Look after yourself today because it won't take much to make you feel flat and lethargic. Perhaps it's just one of those days when your energy levels aren't as high as usual and you need to take things gently? It will certainly do you good to have a rest at some point, even if that means taking the phone off the hook for five minutes and having a power nap at your desk. Try not to push yourself too hard because you simply don't have the stamina right now.

• *Saturday 13 July* •

You're going to be busy behind the scenes during the next few weeks, and there may be reasons why you can't raise your profile higher. Perhaps you'll be working as someone's back-up team, so they take all the glory and you do most of the hard work. Or maybe you just want to stay out of the limelight at the moment because it's easier that way? At times you may struggle to stay motivated, but you will have to force yourself over major issues.

• *Sunday 14 July* •

It's a day for letting your hair down and enjoying yourself, preferably in the company of friends. It's one of those lovely occasions when everyone gets on well with everyone else with no effort at all. You might even add a new name to your list of friends because there's a good chance that you'll make some new contacts right now. If you're taking part in a group event you'll really stand out from the crowd.

• *Monday 15 July* •

This is another day when friends are wonderful company. They'll take you out of yourself if you're feeling a bit down, and give you even more to feel good about if you're already feeling happy. So you'll win either way! The only possible snag is that you might spend too much money because you get carried away and can't say no. But think of the fun you'll have in the process!

• *Tuesday 16 July* •

Mind how you go when mixing friends and finances today, because they could easily curdle. A certain person could get into a bit of a snit over money, perhaps because they're envious of someone else's good fortune or they just can't resist making a few sly digs. If you're trying to organize a big social event for lots of friends, you'll need plenty of patience now to deal with all their different ideas and suggestions. Everyone will be convinced that they're right and the rest of the gang are wrong!

• *Wednesday 17 July* •

Once again you should be careful about combining money and friends, especially if there's still a bad atmosphere after yesterday's events. It might all erupt in a row or a big showdown, but at least you'll get the chance to have your say. If you're busy working on a project for the future, you might hit a snag when someone prevents you doing what you want or you realize you're short of funds. Take things gently and don't panic.

• *Thursday 18 July* •

Social events are great fun today, so try not to spend all your time by yourself. Apart from the enjoyment you'll have, it would be a shame to deprive everyone of your company! It looks as though you're in the mood to go shopping, and you'll certainly enjoy seeing what's on offer. Why not take someone along to keep you company, so you can go out for a drink or some food once you're finished?

• *Friday 19 July* •

Things are looking up! You're in a buoyant mood today and you want to get the most out of the day. It's a marvellous chance to push ahead with your long-term plans and wishes because you're keen to make things happen and you're in the mood to work hard at them. Group activities are a real pleasure now, particularly if you can be with like-minded people. It's even better if you're taking charge of the proceedings because everything will go like clockwork.

• *Saturday 20 July* •

You're still wrapped up in your plans for the future, and today you've got some really big ideas. You're not prepared to be limited by other people's ideas of what's possible and what isn't – you want to prove something to yourself and you're determined to give it your best shot. There is so much that you're capable of right now that you don't want to turn down any ideas or restrict yourself in any way. Even a miracle might happen now!

• *Sunday 21 July* •

Speaking up for yourself won't be very easy between now and early August. For various reasons you'll feel shy, tongue-tied and reluctant to say what's on your mind. You may not even be completely sure how you feel about certain things, perhaps because you're reluctant to face up to them or because you keep changing your mind. Yet it won't do you much good to bottle things up if they're bothering you, so find a confidant you can trust.

• *Monday 22 July* •

Even if you're the sort of Virgo who prides themselves on being rational and pragmatic, things don't exactly work out that way today. Your emotions are never far from the surface and as a result you'll be susceptible to all sorts of feelings that you may usually dismiss as feeble, sentimental or indulgent. Well, it's a day to acknowledge all those emotions that you usually firmly keep under wraps! Watching a weepie film might help to bring buried feelings to the surface without them interfering with the rest of your day.

• *Tuesday 23 July* •

You've been feeling very dynamic recently but from today you really start to climb into your shell and you won't fully emerge until late August. This is a marvellous opportunity for you to recharge your batteries after all your recent exploits, and just to take things easy for a while. You don't have to put your entire life on hold but a few early nights might do you the world of good!

• *Wednesday 24 July* •

Emotional situations threaten to get out of hand today because a certain someone doesn't know when to control themselves and rein in their feelings. Unfortunately, you may also find it hard to gain mastery over your emotions, especially if you're dealing with situations that feel as though your very survival is at stake. Be very careful not to use emotional blackmail to get your own way because it won't go down at all well.

• *Thursday 25 July* •

This is a rather strange day. You're brimming with ideas and you've got lots of energy, but it's difficult to express these feelings. Perhaps that's because you're in an inappropriate setting and you've got to keep your head down, or maybe you simply feel it isn't the right time to speak up. Even so, try to burn off your nervous energy in positive ways, otherwise you'll feel very jittery by the end of the day.

• *Friday 26 July* •

Don't believe everything you hear today. Someone may be fudging the issue for their own benefit or they may be trying to protect your feelings by keeping the truth from you. Whatever's going on, you need a hefty pinch of salt on standby at all times! If you're at work and you're on the carpet for something you've done wrong, it will be far better to admit to your mistake than to try to cover it up and pretend it's nothing to do with you. Your little white lies will be found out so you may as well come clean straight away!

• *Saturday 27 July* •

It's horribly easy to get yourself in a state over things today. Once that happens, you'll struggle to keep a grip on yourself and it won't be long before you start a scene or make other people feel uncomfortable. That may be exactly what's needed, especially if you're feeling upset about something and you need to clear the air. But even so, try to resist the temptation to create a massive crisis out of a tiny problem. Keep things in proportion!

• *Sunday 28 July* •

Conserve your energy today otherwise you'll run out of it before you're ready to down tools. If you've started the day feeling below par or lacking in fizz, it will be even more important for you to pace yourself. It might also help to practise some creative visualization or any other technique that will use the power of your mind to make you feel better. You'll be astonished by the positive results!

• *Monday 29 July* •

This is a marvellous day for zeroing in on important issues and making sure you understand exactly what's involved. Your mind is razor-sharp now and you want to get at the facts, especially if you suspect they've been hidden beneath a pile of excuses or a cloud of hot air. This is also a good day to have a blitz on any clutter you've accumulated at home. Do you really need to keep it or would you feel better if you could get shot of it?

• *Tuesday 30 July* •

Look into your joint and official money matters today, just to make sure that everything is progressing according to plan. You might decide to check out the different interest rates offered by the various credit card companies, in case you're paying over the odds and could make a saving. If you pool your money into a kitty with someone, check that things are running smoothly and that neither of you has any hidden objections to the way everything is organized.

• *Wednesday 31 July* •

You're in a very businesslike mood today and you don't want to hang around wasting time. You'd much rather get on with whatever is important, do it properly, and then move on to the next thing. No wonder people are looking at you in such a favourable light! If you behave like this around a boss or superior, they may start to wonder whether you deserve a pat on the back or even a promotion. You already know that, of course, but it seems they've been a bit slow on the uptake!

AUGUST AT A GLANCE

Love	♥ ♥ ♥ ♥ ♥
Money	£ $ £
Career	💻 💻 💻
Health	☼ ☼ ☼ ☼ ☼

• *Thursday 1 August* •

The background picture starts to change today because over the next few months you'll get a strong sense that your guardian angel is looking after your interests and making sure you're OK. This doesn't mean that you should take foolish risks but you do have a safety net and very often you'll manage to escape from tricky situations by the skin of your teeth. You may also find that certain people are most definitely on your side right now. Maybe they're angels in human form?

• *Friday 2 August* •

Just when you're riding high, someone takes a pin and bursts your bubble. That's exactly how you feel today, thanks to the miserable or depressing behaviour of a certain person. If you really care about them, you may start to fret because you feel there's a huge gulf separating the two of you. If you work for them, they may give you a rather frosty reception. It won't take much to scare yourself about what's going on but the whole episode may blow over, so don't press the panic button yet.

• *Saturday 3 August* •

There's a lot you can achieve today, although you'll fare best if you can be left to your own devices without many interruptions from other people. If you're busy at work it might be a good idea to hang a sign on your door saying 'Do not disturb' or to switch on the answering machine so you can have a clear run at what you're doing. It's also a good day for uncovering secrets and getting down to the truth.

• *Sunday 4 August* •

Anything goes today, so be prepared! The best way to handle today's disruptive and unpredictable events is to go with the flow whenever possible, otherwise you'll soon wind yourself up like a spring. Speaking of winding up, watch out for someone whose idea of fun is to tease you without letting on that that's what they're doing. They'll get you into a right old state unless you cotton on. Keep your sense of humour – you'll need it!

• *Monday 5 August* •

Women are rather difficult customers today, so you need to tread carefully around them. They may be uncooperative or one woman may set herself up in competition with you, creating a nasty atmosphere in the process. It may also be tough keeping an older female relative or friend happy, especially if she's in a huffy mood or is taking offence at the slightest little thing. Yikes! Don't worry, things will soon get back to normal.

• *Tuesday 6 August* •

You've been uncharacteristically silent recently but you're starting to feel more chatty from today. And about time, too! You may have a few words to say to certain people, especially if you're fed up with the way they've been behaving recently. Between now and late August you'll be very wrapped up in your own thoughts and will be reluctant to talk about much else, but try not to hog the conversation all the time or you'll end up talking to thin air because everyone will have left you to it!

• *Wednesday 7 August* •

From today you have a real appreciation of the good things in life. Over the next four weeks you'll really enjoy indulging yourself in little pleasures and treats, even if you're usually the sort of Virgo who slightly disapproves of such things. Of course, all this will probably cost you money but you'll want to invest in items that give you pleasure. If you've got the cash, this is the perfect opportunity to buy something that will grow in value as well as make you happy every time you look at it.

• *Thursday 8 August* •

Worries are never far from your thoughts but over the next two weeks you've got the chance to face up to certain fears and banish them from your mind. If you do this, you may discover that you've been fretting over nothing, because when you analyse it in the cold light of day you'll realize it's all a figment of your imagination. Even if you're anxious about something that's very real, try limiting your worrying time to a few minutes a day and then force yourself to think about more positive things. It could make a big difference to your mental outlook.

• *Friday 9 August* •

If you've got a busy schedule today you're going to need lots of patience to deal with the interruptions and disruptions that are almost bound to occur. Try to build in extra time if you're doing something important, to allow for things to go wrong. If you don't, you'll end up feeling like a complete nervous wreck. It will also help to check that important appliances and machines are running properly, to reduce the possibility of them letting you down when you need them most.

• *Saturday 10 August* •

After yesterday's tensions you need to let off steam! Even punching a cushion in the privacy of your own room will help you to get rid of pent-up frustration, especially if there are reasons why you can't do anything more public than this. It's also a good day to work on some exciting plans, even if you can't put them into action yet. It's enough to map out your strategy at the moment.

• *Sunday 11 August* •

Your confidence takes a bit of a nosedive today, so be prepared. You may worry that you can't measure up to what other people expect of you, or you could feel defeated by the mound of work that's waiting for you. Unfortunately, it won't help that you're so quick to find fault with yourself and place the blame squarely on your own shoulders if things go wrong. Stop being so self-critical and remind yourself of some of your recent triumphs.

• *Monday 12 August* •

Your health means a lot to you and today is a good chance to spend some money on maintaining it. You might decide to buy some vitamins or minerals to supplement your diet, especially if it isn't as nutritious as you'd like. Or you might simply decide to buy a piece of fruit instead of that chocolate bar you've got your eye on. Something else that might appeal is treating yourself to some aromatherapy oils or anything else that smells good and does you good at the same time.

• *Tuesday 13 August* •

A charity or good cause appeals to you today. You like the idea of helping people who are having a hard time and you'll do what you can to support them. Or maybe you're thinking about donating your services in some other way, such as taking part in a voluntary scheme? Alternatively, you may decide that charity begins at home, in which case you'll want to keep a close eye on anyone who's been going through the mill recently.

• *Wednesday 14 August* •

Someone's got a lot to say for themselves! If you're the chatterbox, you'll enjoy nattering about whatever pops into your head to whoever happens to be around at the time. You won't get much work done but you'll certainly have a good time! It's the perfect excuse to pick up the phone and make contact with people you haven't seen in a while, or maybe it would be cheaper to send them a newsy letter?

• *Thursday 15 August* •

It's difficult to maintain your objectivity today because your emotions keep getting in the way. As a result, you may get a bee in your bonnet about something and find it almost impossible to switch off and think about anything else. Try to distract yourself otherwise you'll end up going round in circles. Alternatively, you'll have to deal with someone who's starting to sound like a broken record because there's only one thing they want to talk about.

• *Friday 16 August* •

If you've had your eye on someone you know through work, you'll have high hopes of them today. What's more, they may make your dreams come true! There's definitely a romantic flavour to your job and your daily routine right now, and you may have stars in your eyes when you're supposed to be getting down to some hard work. You might also be smitten by someone, such as a doctor or nurse, that you meet through a medical matter.

• *Saturday 17 August* •

You hanker for familiar faces and places today because they'll make you happiest. It's the perfect excuse to gather the family around you or to get in lots of food and have open house. You'll really enjoy catering for everyone, making sure they're happy and well fed. If that sounds too ambitious, you'll enjoy relaxing at home, taking life easy and chatting to whoever happens to be around.

• *Sunday 18 August* •

Creative activities are highly enjoyable today. It will do you good to work on projects that allow you to express yourself. Don't imagine that you've got to do something wildly ambitious, such as your own version of painting the Sistine Chapel or writing an entire novel, otherwise it won't count. Choose an activity that is so enjoyable it's almost like second nature. It might be pottering about in the garden, baking a cake or playing with a child. It will be a great way to unwind.

• *Monday 19 August* •

You're in a very constructive and organized mood today. You know exactly what you want to achieve and you also know that you're going to do it. It will help if you can plan your time in advance, so you don't have to repeat any activities and there's no danger of discovering you're doing things in the wrong order. Simply knowing that you're doing something to the best of your ability will fill you with satisfaction.

• *Tuesday 20 August* •

You long to break out of your rut today! And the more restrictive, predictable or tedious this rut is, the more desperate you'll be to escape from it. Try to take positive action before you reach screaming point, otherwise you'll do something rash or foolhardy. If it's your job that's slowly driving you batty, maybe it's time to look for something else, especially if you know you're wasting your talents at the moment. Today you have a strong sense that life is too short to do things that aren't right for you.

• *Wednesday 21 August* •

Don't underestimate your abilities today because you can achieve a tremendous amount, especially where your work is concerned. If you can find a way of combining tradition and innovation, you'll find a marvellous key to future success. For instance, if you're considering switching careers this is a good chance to think about which areas of experience you can build on and which ones you should jettison in order to start again from scratch.

• *Thursday 22 August* •

Pay close attention to household budgets and domestic expenses today. You'll find it very satisfying to go through everything in a lot of detail, particularly if you're looking for ways to cut down on your outgoings. This is also a good day to talk about old times with someone who shared them with you. You're feeling pleasantly nostalgic and will enjoy a sentimental wander down memory lane.

• *Friday 23 August* •

You've been taking a back seat in life recently but you really want to emerge from your shell from today. The coming month will see you busily engaged on all sorts of personal projects and innovations. It will also be a time when you enjoy a lot more confidence than you've experienced lately, so it's great for having the courage to stand out from the crowd or do something that requires some bravado.

• *Saturday 24 August* •

Tasks and responsibilities weigh heavily on you today. They may even threaten to weigh you down, making you feel burdened by the duties that other people have foisted on you. If it's all getting a bit too much, maybe you should say so? It's all very well taking on extra work and soldiering through it, but that's no good if you're going to end up feeling exhausted because you're working right round the clock. If you do that, you won't perform in the way you wish and you may even end up disappointing everyone else as well as yourself.

• *Sunday 25 August* •

You're feeling nicely industrious today without making yourself jump through hoops. You know exactly what you're capable of and you'll stick at it until you achieve what you set out to do. If possible, try to work by yourself because that's the best way to concentrate now. Activities connected with charities and voluntary groups also go well, and you'll have a strong urge to make a difference to someone's life or to publicize your campaign.

• *Monday 26 August* •

Start thinking about your finances from today, especially if they've been a little lacklustre lately. Over the next few weeks you should go into all your money matters in great detail, making sure you know what's what. Check your bank statements to make sure that all your transactions have gone through properly. If you always seem to run at a loss, try to work out a realistic budget that stops you being in the red all the time.

• *Tuesday 27 August* •

If you're wondering what to do in your job or your career, consider talking to someone who's got plenty of experience. You'll appreciate having their input, even if you don't agree with everything they say. This is also a good day to work hard at establishing a stronger bond with a partner. This might be your other half or it could be someone you work with. What's important is to establish a feeling of trust between the two of you.

• *Wednesday 28 August* •

Life has so much to offer today that you don't know where to start. You feel spoiled for choice! If you keep your eyes peeled you might spot some wonderful opportunities that come along, but you'll have to act quickly if you want to snap them up! You also need to keep an open mind because some of the chances that arrive may not seem all that good at first. It's only later on that you'll realize how much they've got to offer.

• *Thursday 29 August* •

Your energy levels rise steeply today, making you bounce about like nobody's business over the next few weeks. Other people will only be able to watch you with envy as you dash around, full of enthusiasm and vitality. If your job means you lead quite a sedentary life, this is your chance to introduce more activity into your daily routine. Maybe you fancy joining a gym or getting up earlier each morning so you can jog round the block before starting work? No, this isn't a joke!

• *Friday 30 August* •

It won't take much to get steam coming out of your ears today. Your patience is wearing very thin at work, particularly if you're in charge of other people and they aren't pulling their weight. You'll quickly point out their failings to them and you may do it in rather a loud voice! Try to control your temper – otherwise you'll end the day bellowing at all and sundry, which will wear you out and make everyone very wary of you.

• *Saturday 31 August* •

Once again you're feeling irascible and bad-tempered. The problems you faced yesterday may still be bugging you, in which case you're ready to put your foot down and take serious action. Even if you know you have to raise the roof, don't do it to such an extent that the plaster will still be falling from the ceiling this time tomorrow. Make your point but don't labour it, otherwise it will lose its effectiveness.

SEPTEMBER AT A GLANCE

Love	♥ ♥ ♥ ♥
Money	£ $ £ $ £
Career	💻 💻
Health	☼ ☼ ☼ ☼ ☼

• *Sunday 1 September* •

Even though this is officially the day of rest, that's not what you're in the mood for. You don't want to be lazy because that feels like a waste of time right now. Instead, you want to do something productive and worthwhile. That's very commendable but you need to remember two things. First of all, don't wear yourself out working round the clock. Secondly, what does the rest of the family think about this? Don't be surprised if they're disappointed and they show it.

• *Monday 2 September* •

Put on your thinking cap today and you'll come up with some very bright ideas about your finances. You might hit on a surefire way of making more money, or you could discover an investment opportunity that seems too good to miss. Even if the prospects look great, try to remember to check them out before rushing into them head first. You're so busy concentrating on the advantages of what you're proposing that you're forgetting to look at the snags.

• *Tuesday 3 September* •

Are you ready for some surprise good news? You could hear something to your advantage at work, such as the fact that a pay rise, perk or bonus is on the way. A satisfied customer might give you a bigger tip than you were expecting. They might also surprise you by making a pass at you or asking you out. There may also be a sudden attraction between you and a colleague, particularly if you've never really fancied them in the past. Suddenly, they seem irresistible!

• *Wednesday 4 September* •

Make the most of your imagination today because it will come up trumps. Although you'll be able to concentrate on fiddly ideas and complex details if you have to, you'll feel far more comfortable letting your mind wander and having some creative daydreams. Believe it or not, staring into space for half an hour could be a lot more productive than reading reports or compiling columns of figures. It's certainly worth a try!

• *Thursday 5 September* •

A certain person is a tower of strength today. You love knowing that you can rely on them, especially if they're giving you some advice or they're there if you need them. This is a lovely day to be with an older friend or relative because you'll feel comforted by their presence. They may also help you to put current problems into perspective or regale you with stories of how they faced similar difficulties and won through.

• *Friday 6 September* •

The last thing you want to do today is sit and watch the grass grow. You're raring to go and want to be on the move whenever possible. You've got so much energy to burn right now that you need to start immediately. How about leaving the car at home and cycling or walking to work? Or maybe you've got a sudden urge to visit the gym and work up a sweat? Watch out when making personal decisions because it will be tempting to reach hasty conclusions that have little to do with the facts.

• *Saturday 7 September* •

If you're still toying with the idea of starting a new health regime but not much has happened so far, let today's New Moon jog your memory. It's giving you the green light for any projects or enterprises that will eventually lead to a brand-new you. You might decide to begin modestly by introducing some minor changes, or maybe you want to go the whole hog right from the start? Of course, life may take matters out of your hands and propel you straight into something new, so be prepared!

• *Sunday 8 September* •

Over the next few weeks you'll really enjoy meeting and mixing with people. Whether they're complete strangers or people you see every day, you'll always find something to say to them. This is a lovely chance to get involved in local activities and neighbourhood projects, particularly if you've recently moved to a new home and you don't yet know many people. It could turn out to be a lot more enjoyable than you expected!

• *Monday 9 September* •

If you're wondering where all your money goes to because you never seem to have any, this is a good day to find out what's going on. Jot down all your weekly expenses, from the major outgoings to the minor ones such as your evening paper. It will give you a good idea of your spending patterns and also show you where to trim your expenses if need be. You may realize that you're frittering away a lot of cash on things you don't really need or want.

• *Tuesday 10 September* •

If a neighbour or close relative has been a pain in the neck recently, you'll find the perfect way to deal with them today. Maybe you want to tick them off or give them a piece of your mind? If so, you'll be able to make your point without making a huge song and dance about it at the same time. Phew, what a relief! If you've got the urge to go shopping, you'll be ready to shop till you drop if necessary. You certainly have a lot of stamina today.

• *Wednesday 11 September* •

This isn't a good day to take risks because you could incur big losses or a lot of disappointment. If you've been taking a slapdash attitude to your work, you might come a cropper now when you're finally rumbled. And if you've been burning the candle at both ends for too long, you could start to feel ill or worn out. If you've been unrealistic about your job prospects or your enjoyment at work, the scales will fall from your eyes now. It will be difficult, but once you know the truth you'll be able to start putting things right.

• *Thursday 12 September* •

If yesterday's events left you shaken and stirred, it's hardly surprising that you're still suffering from the after-effects. You're feeling vulnerable, slightly defensive and a bit on the scratchy side. However, it won't help if you take your bad mood out on everyone around you because they'll soon lose their sympathy for you. You'll also end up making yourself feel thoroughly miserable and your popularity will take a nosedive.

• *Friday 13 September* •

If you've been stewing about something recently but haven't managed to get it off your chest, watch out for what happens today. Pent-up feelings will soon rise to the surface, forcing you to acknowledge them. You might feel tearful, argumentative or sentimental, depending on what's bugging you. You may also find yourself harking back to past slights and insults, and feeling aggrieved about things that are now ancient history. Deal with your current problems and let sleeping dogs lie.

• *Saturday 14 September* •

During the rest of September it won't always be easy to keep track of what's happening to your finances. You may be given some misleading information or the facts may be unavailable at the time. For instance, if you phone your bank to check the balance of your current account, you may be told that the computer's down and you'll have to ring back. Doublecheck any invoices or bills that arrive in case they contain mistakes or oversights.

• *Sunday 15 September* •

The more energy you put into the day, the more you'll get out of it. So don't sit back expecting everyone else to do all the hard work while you take things easy! You'll have great fun playing with children and larking about, and you won't even end up in an exhausted heap at the end of it! It's a super day for trying out your skills in a competitive sport too, because you'll have the killer instinct and want to win. Good luck!

• *Monday 16 September* •

Life continues to be good fun today. You're definitely in the mood to enjoy yourself right now so try to put the chores aside until tomorrow if possible. Creative and artistic activities will bring out the best in you now, whether you're the one who's doing all the work or you're admiring someone else's talents. For instance, how about a trip to the cinema or theatre? Or if you've always fancied the idea of being on the stage, why not find out if there's a drama or music group in your area? Go on, be adventurous!

• *Tuesday 17 September* •

This is the day to tackle all the work you postponed from yesterday. You'll enjoy plodding away at it, provided you give yourself lots of mini breaks to avoid getting bored or stale. A colleague is good company now although they may get carried away emotionally at times. Maybe you need to keep them calm. Or perhaps all they want is to tell you their troubles and then they'll feel better?

• *Wednesday 18 September* •

Does life feel rather predictable today? Then try to ring the changes in some way, otherwise you'll end up feeling stifled and hemmed in. These changes don't have to be very dramatic or big to make a difference to your mood. Even varying the time when you take your coffee break, or going somewhere else for lunch, might be enough to give your routine some extra spice. One word of warning – your energy levels may be rather erratic, so try to make allowances in whatever you're doing.

• *Thursday 19 September* •

The higher you raise your hopes today, the more likely they are to be dashed. Remember that, if you've been looking forward to something all week and now it's arrived. Your heightened sense of anticipation may not live up to reality! If things don't go the way you want, you'll feel cheated and let down. But maybe you were expecting too much in the first place? Try to keep your feet on the ground!

• *Friday 20 September* •

A partner is hard to handle today. They're touchy, grouchy and argumentative, and you're pretty sure that a row is brewing. Rather than tiptoe around them on eggshells, waiting for the bomb to go off, maybe it would be better to get the argument out of the way sooner than later? Ask them what's wrong and suggest that you talk about it. All the same, avoid provoking confrontations and stirring up trouble just to get your own back because it won't do you much good.

• *Saturday 21 September* •

If you're still smarting from yesterday's events, today's Full Moon will make you eager to bring things to a head and do something about them. However, try to start off with a softly-softly approach, because going in with all guns blazing may not help your cause in the long run. It may also leave you without much room for manoeuvre, especially if you want to save face and think that reaching compromises means you're caving in. Don't do anything hasty!

• *Sunday 22 September* •

Stalemate! You come up against the brick wall of someone's stubbornness today, and it seems there's no way round it. This person is determined to stand their ground and not give an inch, and you're probably being equally obstinate even if you aren't prepared to admit it! Neither of you will get anywhere if you carry on like this, so how about backing off and waiting until you're both willing to listen to the other person's argument.

• *Monday 23 September* •

What and who matters most to you in life? These are important questions to ponder during the next four weeks, and you could be surprised by the answers. The next question to ask yourself is whether you devote enough time to these priorities. If you don't, how can you make more room for them in your life? If you've been feeling dissatisfied recently, you may have hit on a way to introduce more meaning into your world.

• *Tuesday 24 September* •

Send your mind on a mini holiday today! Let your thoughts roam in whichever direction they want to take. It will do you the world of good to do some daydreaming or just to forget about the chores for a while. This will allow your intuition to make itself heard and it could send you some very interesting messages. You might have a flash of inspiration about a medical problem, especially if you've been wondering how to solve it or what caused it. Allow your inner voice to speak to you!

• *Wednesday 25 September* •

Thoughts of holidays are whirling round your head today. If you haven't yet taken off on your annual vacation, you'll be champing at the bit right now. That will heighten your expectations if you're currently packing for your trip, but it will make you feel rather restless if your next jaunt is still a long way off. So how are you going to satisfy your need for adventure and fresh horizons? How about planning a weekend break so you've got something to look forward to?

• *Thursday 26 September* •

If you've decided to book up a holiday or long journey, be very careful when making the arrangements today. Watch out for any spur of the moment decisions, because although they seem like a good idea at the time, later on you may wonder what on earth you were thinking of. At work you may have to deal with an unruly colleague who seems hell-bent on creating as much disturbance and agitation as possible. If they seem to thrive on the discord they're causing, don't give them the satisfaction of knowing that they've got to you.

• *Friday 27 September* •

You're currently on a quest to discover what really matters to you in life and this is a good day to continue your search. Talking to someone sympathetic may encourage you to reveal thoughts and feelings that have been hidden from you until now. However, try not to hog the conversation because you may have a tendency to talk the hind legs off a donkey today! Alternatively, how about putting your thoughts down on paper? They could be very enlightening.

• *Saturday 28 September* •

Put on your boxing gloves because you're about to get involved in a fight! With luck it won't develop into fisticuffs but it will still be a free and frank exchange of views. It's good to tell someone how you feel, especially if you're delivering a few home truths, but it might be wise to pull your punches at times and preserve their dignity. Giving someone the verbal equivalent of some knockout punches will only make them more determined to give as good as they get. That's when things will escalate and run the risk of turning nasty.

• *Sunday 29 September* •

Someone's got out of bed the wrong side today. What a weekend this is turning out to be! Luckily it isn't as bad-tempered a day as yesterday, but you'll still have to deal with someone who's being grumpy. If you want to keep the atmosphere as friendly as possible, avoid mixing business and pleasure or love and money. They're a fast track to trouble right now and will give someone an excuse to feel hard done by or envious.

• *Monday 30 September* •

Thank goodness the month ends on a jolly note! You've had a basinful of problems over the past few days but they've now passed and you want to put them behind you. The best way to do that is to relax, preferably in the company of some good friends or close family. You may even have a good laugh telling them about all your recent adventures. Group activities and hobbies will also help you to unwind now.

OCTOBER AT A GLANCE

Love	♥ ♥ ♥
Money	£ $ £ $ £
Career	💻 💻
Health	☼ ☼ ☼

• *Tuesday 1 October* •

Other people's happiness is uppermost in your mind today. If you know someone who's going through a bad time or isn't very well, you'll feel it's a matter of honour to take care of them now. Be wary if you're sorting out finances connected with your job, such as filling in your expenses form, because there could be some confusion about it. You may also be having second thoughts about your job and wondering whether it's really your cup of tea. Think on.

• *Wednesday 2 October* •

Take care over the next few days because at times it will be hard to keep track of your thoughts, and that could lead to a lot of muddle and confusion. For instance, even though you think you're being articulate and saying things clearly, other people may beg to differ! They may also get the wrong end of the stick because you accidentally forget to mention something rather important. So do your best to leave no room for doubt now.

• *Thursday 3 October* •

If you aren't sure whether you've been doing a job or task properly, this is a good chance to check it over for mistakes. Take it slowly and examine it from every angle. If you're still pondering whether your job is right for you, you'll have more to chew on today. However, bear in mind that you may be feeling slightly pessimistic and taking a rather dim view of things that aren't really as bad as they seem.

• *Friday 4 October* •

Get out that pair of kid gloves! You're going to need it when dealing with certain members of the family. They're spoiling for a fight and it won't help if they're feeling miffed or offended by someone or something. They'll behave as though they have a God-given right to make everyone's life a misery because they're feeling wretched themselves. They'll also wonder why everyone wants to give them a wide berth. Only tell them the truth if you're feeling very brave!

• *Saturday 5 October* •

If you're a bit fed up after yesterday's tensions, you may be feeling rather bolshie yourself now. You may even decide to give someone a piece of your mind. That's a good idea if you've been revving up for a showdown with them and you have a genuine grievance. But try to avoid having one of those days when you nit-pick and squabble with people for no real reason. A little exercise will help to burn off some of your angst.

• *Sunday 6 October* •

Thank goodness communications start to run smoothly again today. This is your chance to pour oil on any troubled waters or to set the record straight with someone. It's also an excellent day for making personal decisions because they stand a good chance of working out well. This is also a great opportunity to discuss subjects that are uppermost in your mind at the moment. Talking about them will help you to work out exactly where you stand.

• *Monday 7 October* •

You certainly aren't afraid of hard work today, which is just as well because it looks as though you'll have rather a lot to deal with! But instead of this being a chore you'll look on it as a cause for satisfaction, because you'll take pride in doing things to the best of your abilities. Someone you respect or admire will be great company and you'll enjoy hearing all about their experiences in the past.

• *Tuesday 8 October* •

Take a look round your home today. Is there room for improvement? Think about what needs to be done and then discuss it with the rest of the family. Maybe you want to do some major renovations or improvements, such as building an extension or converting the loft, or perhaps you're considering doing some redecoration. Whatever plans you have, it's a good day to talk them through and possibly even decide how to finance them.

• *Wednesday 9 October* •

Someone's in a very serious mood today. They're probably pulling rather a long face and keep finding fault with everything. Or are you the one who's feeling gloomy and is doused in pessimism? If so, try not to brood on anything that's currently bothering you or you'll soon start to feel that the situation is completely hopeless and you might as well give up right now. It's unlikely that things are as bad as they seem.

• *Thursday 10 October* •

If you're still thinking about the plans you began to hatch on Tuesday, carry on the good work today. Gather the family together for a pow-wow, or talk to them on the phone and see what they think. It's important to get other people's views because they could have some good ideas and they'll also appreciate being consulted. And, of course, if they live with you, it's only good manners to see what they think about the changes you're planning to their home.

• *Friday 11 October* •

In late August and early September you spent a lot of time thinking about your finances and finding ways to improve things, but then you were interrupted. But from today until the end of the month you're in a great position to continue all that good work and see exactly where you stand financially. You may already have done all the research you need, so now you're ready to swing into action. Play your cards right and you could be better off by Christmas!

• *Saturday 12 October* •

Whatever else you have planned today, make sure you enjoy yourself at some point. You're in a very easy-going and amiable mood, and you want to spread a little sunshine wherever you go. One of the venues you've got in mind is the shops, because you love the idea of browsing and spending a little money now. Another possible destination is your favourite restaurant or café, for some edible delights.

• *Sunday 13 October* •

Feelings run high today and it won't help that certain people seem determined to turn molehills into mountains. They're getting over-emotional and melodramatic, and it will be exhausting to be around them for any length of time. You may also lose your temper with them and want to tell them to grow up. If you've just bought something expensive it's not a good idea to flaunt it because that's guaranteed to put someone's nose out of joint. Keep quiet about it for the time being.

• *Monday 14 October* •

You'll need plenty of patience to cope with today's frustrating atmosphere. You'll feel as though you're banging your head against a brick wall, when things don't go the way you want.

You may even have to deal with someone who is apparently deliberately being obstructive or unhelpful. It's a waste of energy trying to get them to play ball and it may be better to let them stew in their own juice for the moment.

• *Tuesday 15 October* •

Your interest in money matters takes another step up the ladder from today, and over the next few weeks you'll be devoting a lot of energy to making your money stretch further. This will be very important to you, especially if you're fed up with trying to make ends meet at the moment, but do your best not to place so much emphasis on the material side of life that you forget about everything else.

• *Wednesday 16 October* •

Roll up your sleeves and get down to whatever work is waiting for you! You'll take great pleasure in doing it to the best of your ability, and it will be a bonus if a boss or superior is looking on in an impressed sort of way. If you're still thinking hard about changing jobs, you'll hear something very useful today. You might also make some good contacts or consider joining an employment agency that specializes in your field.

• *Thursday 17 October* •

Enjoyment comes top of your list of priorities today. In fact, you won't have much time or patience for anything else! This is a wonderful day for forgetting all about the chores and doing whatever makes you feel good instead. You may have to do this in a rather subtle way, especially if someone is waiting for you to do lots of work! There may also be an element of secrecy in what you get up to now – perhaps you're getting together with someone who you're not supposed to be with?

• *Friday 18 October* •

You're very tuned in to other people today, so put your ESP to good use. You might realize that a colleague is feeling miserable without them having to say a word, or you could have fun when talking to someone because you both seem able to read the other one's mind. If someone is having a bad time, you'll be the first person they turn to for help because they'll know instinctively that you're feeling sympathetic and compassionate.

• *Saturday 19 October* •

Keep a firm grip on your money today otherwise it will fly about in all directions like confetti. Impulse buys are almost irresistible, although you may wonder why you bothered when you get them home. Unfortunately money could also cause a problem between you and a certain person, especially if you pool your resources in some way. A row could flare up because one of you objects to the way the other is spending money, and it will be easy to get things out of proportion.

• *Sunday 20 October* •

You're in a much more easy-going mood today and you're also feeling big enough to say sorry if need be. You realize that there's nothing to be gained from holding on to grievances and resentments, because the only person who's damaged by them is you. So give your partner a big hug and a kiss, then put the entire episode behind you. You have more important things to do today, such as enjoy yourself whenever you get the chance!

• *Monday 21 October* •

If money worries are still preying on your mind, let today's Full Moon help you to sort things out over the coming fortnight. The first thing to do is to sort out your priorities, so write down lists of your income and outgoings so that you know exactly where you stand. It may also help to consult an expert, especially if you're considering making big changes such as switching your mortgage or taking out a pension.

• *Tuesday 22 October* •

This is a wonderfully industrious day and you're keen to make the most of it. You'll certainly live up to your astrological reputation for being a hard worker and someone who doesn't shirk their responsibilities. But don't imagine that you'll have your nose to the grindstone all day long. You may also get the chance to have a valuable talk with someone who can help you to make a success of your life, or who has the contacts that you need to get in touch with.

• *Wednesday 23 October* •

Those domestic ideas that you were mulling over at the start of the month are once again occupying your thoughts. Have another look at your plans and see whether they're feasible. You may even want to take things one step further and start working out a budget that won't break the bank. Or maybe you fancy a trip to a DIY shop or a showroom so you can see what's on offer? This is a project that's really starting to appeal to you!

• *Thursday 24 October* •

You're fired with enthusiasm today, especially when it comes to your career and long-term plans. You're determined to achieve something right now, even if it seems a very modest success by other people's standards. For instance, you might be pleased with yourself because you tick off every item on that list of things to do. Or maybe you grit your teeth and force yourself to do something that you've been putting off for ages. It will be much easier than you imagined!

• *Friday 25 October* •

Take cover! A loved one is getting themselves into a right old state and you're likely to be in the firing line. They've got an axe to grind and they won't be satisfied until they've made everyone else thoroughly miserable. Sadly, you may also be infected by this vengeful mood, especially if you start to think about events that happened a long time ago in which you came off badly. But what's the point in that? You'll only make yourself angry and it's far too late to do anything about the past, so don't waste your time.

• *Saturday 26 October* •

There's a lot of fun to be had today, especially if you can get together with friends and family. It's the perfect opportunity to call a truce over any squabbles or spats that have sprung up recently and to allow peace to break out in all its glory. If you're going out on the town you'll want to have as good a time as possible. A group activity or favourite hobby is also very enjoyable now, and it might even introduce you to some kindred spirits you've never met before.

• *Sunday 27 October* •

What happens today will have a very significant impact on you over the next few months. It's a terrific day for being willing to make big changes to your life, especially where your home, family and the past are concerned. You might decide to let sleeping dogs lie if you've been considering complaining about something, or you may start to feel very contented and happy with your life. If you're about to move house, it will be a very important event for you.

• *Monday 28 October* •

Your brain is buzzing with good ideas today, so keep track of as many as possible. This may not always be as easy as it sounds because your mind is working so fast that ideas will come and go in no time at all. Don't be shy about being innovative and wanting to tackle schemes that seem a bit risky. You're keen to strike out in new directions now, combining the benefits of all your experience with the excitement of starting something completely different.

• *Tuesday 29 October* •

Niggles and petty irritations really get to you today. Even if you usually pride yourself on taking things calmly and rationally, you aren't nearly as cool-headed right now. You may have to deal with someone who irritates you at the best of times but nearly drives you to distraction at the moment. Is that because they're being extra annoying or because you're not as patient as usual? Go for a brisk walk or pound the stuffing out of the punch bag in the gym if necessary, rather than yell at people who don't really deserve it.

• *Wednesday 30 October* •

If you really lost your rag yesterday you'll be feeling disappointed with yourself today. You may even be castigating yourself for not having behaved better or for not having superhuman reserves of patience and understanding. This is the sort of day when you feel bad about yourself because you aren't a saint or a shining example of humanity. Apologize if need be and learn from what happened.

• *Thursday 31 October* •

You're in a very talkative mood today and you'll stay this way for most of the next three weeks. It's a great chance to chat away to whoever happens to be around, because you'll be interested in what they have to say and you'll also want to talk about whatever happens to be on your mind at the time. Your phone bill might shoot up now or you might spend more time on the Internet because of your desire to keep in touch with everyone. If you're flat broke, perhaps you'd better write lots of letters instead!

NOVEMBER AT A GLANCE

Love	♥ ♥
Money	£ $ £
Career	💻 💻
Health	☼ ☼

• *Friday 1 November* •

It's a low-key start to the month because you're feeling a bit tired and fed up. You may also be suffering from a big attack of pessimism, and all you can do is ride it out and wait for it to pass. If you're feeling as though you've got the cares of the world on your shoulders, it's highly likely that things aren't nearly as doom-laden as they seem. Spend today doing something that you're good at, so you can feel pleased with yourself.

• *Saturday 2 November* •

Money burns a big hole in your pocket today! Even if you can barely rub two halfpennies together at the moment, you're keen to go shopping now. It's a great day for striking a bargain or doing some serious haggling because you're determined not to give in until you get what you want. You may also consider spending money on your car or another form of transport, especially if you're buying something that will make it go faster!

• *Sunday 3 November* •

Whatever else you have planned for today, try to fit in a few minutes to go over your finances in detail. Check recent bank or credit card statements to make sure they don't contain any mistakes. It's also a good day for having a domestic turnout. If you dread to think what's lurking at the back of the fridge because it's such a long time since you cleaned it out, steel yourself to have a blitz on it now.

• *Monday 4 November* •

It's time to start a new chapter in your relationship with someone who you see on a regular basis. If you've been taking them for granted recently, you now need to view them in a fresh light. This is an especially good opportunity to clear the air with a neighbour or close member of the family. You're ready to talk things through in a rational way, and to agree to differ if necessary. After all, who's to say who's right and who's wrong?

• *Tuesday 5 November* •

If you're planning to celebrate Bonfire Night with a party, be prepared for a certain someone to act like a damp squib. Maybe they don't feel very well or perhaps they're just being a killjoy, but they won't be the life and soul of the party you were hoping for. Keep track of paperwork today otherwise it will be irritatingly elusive. You may put something down in one place only to have it seemingly disappear before your very eyes, so you have to spend hours searching for it. The more distracted you are, the worse this will be, so concentrate!

• *Wednesday 6 November* •

The thought of being busy doing nothing is very attractive right now! You're very tempted to put your feet up and let the rest of the world carry on without you. Well, what's to stop you? Try to postpone as many chores as possible, or how about delegating them? Even if there's no escaping plenty of work, try to relax at home at some point. Simple pleasures go a long way now, such as eating your favourite meal while watching your favourite TV programme. Heaven!

• *Thursday 7 November* •

Your emotions take an intense turn today, making you react far more strongly to things than usual. But try not to go overboard and turn everything into a drama, otherwise you'll wear yourself out! If you're getting fed up with tripping over things at home because the place is untidy or you've accumulated a lot of clutter recently, this is a good day to have a massive tidy up and to throw out all those things you don't need any longer.

• *Friday 8 November* •

Life feels rather like drudgery today. You may also be feeling a little antisocial. Perhaps you've got a pile of work to get through and you're wondering how you'll cope, or you're dealing with someone for whom nothing is ever quite good enough. Whatever's wrong, it will get you down if you let it so try to find something that will cheer you up. You will also find it easier if you can work on your own rather than have to cope with other people's demands and chatter.

• *Saturday 9 November* •

In sharp contrast to yesterday, you're now feeling much more positive. That comes as a big relief and you may even be wondering why you got so stewed up yesterday. What a difference a day makes! But it's more than that because you're also seeing things in a much more positive light and you're determined to concentrate on your strengths rather than your weaknesses. You know what you can do and you're keen to prove it.

• *Sunday 10 November* •

You have the power! You have bags of will power and decisiveness today, and you know exactly what you're doing. This is a fantastic chance to make some positive changes to your life, particularly where your finances and home are concerned. You're now aware of the areas that need your attention and you're willing to do whatever is necessary to make them more fulfilling and satisfactory. What's more, you're eager to involve everyone else in your decisions and that's exactly the way it should be right now.

• *Monday 11 November* •

Everything's looking good! You're feeling very sure of yourself without being bumptious or overbearing. It's a marvellous day for tackling your finances, particularly if you want to swell the coffers. For instance, you might decide to make some long-term investments. If you're wondering how to make ends meet, this is a good opportunity to investigate benefits and allowances that you may be entitled to. You've got the energy to charge through all that red tape and get to the facts.

• *Tuesday 12 November* •

Your social life is looking good! You're feeling very considerate towards other people and you'll do whatever you can to put them at their ease. If a little diplomacy is called for with a certain someone, you'll manage it with no trouble at all because you'll know exactly what to say to sweeten them up. But even though your policy is anything for a quiet life today, don't agree to any demands that will make a rod for your own back in the long run. It's important not to be a doormat.

• *Wednesday 13 November* •

Relationships are still going strong and once again you're eager to keep everyone happy. If they've got any sense they'll really appreciate the efforts you're making on their behalf. This is one of those happy days when you find it easy to get on with whoever you're with. One-to-one relationships will be especially harmonious because you're at such pains to put everyone at their ease.

• *Thursday 14 November* •

Tact and charm flow out of you like honey today. If someone shows signs of losing their temper or going into a huff, you'll soon manage to smooth their ruffled feathers and get them back on an even keel. But try not to spend the entire day troubleshooting because there's a lot of enjoyment to be had. Get together with close friends or family and go out for a night on the tiles. You've earned it!

• *Friday 15 November* •

A certain person isn't exactly a bundle of laughs today. Quite the reverse, in fact, because they're about as much fun as a wet weekend. If you spend too long in their company you'll also start to feel like a right old misery, so ration the time you share with them. This isn't a good day to make exciting suggestions to anyone because they're more likely to pour cold water on them than to give them the go-ahead. Wait until a day when the atmosphere is more positive.

• *Saturday 16 November* •

It's difficult to concentrate on anything for long today because your mind keeps straying off on to different subjects. That's fine if you don't have a deadline looming but it will be very irritating if you're trying to focus on something because the clock is ticking and you can't get on with it. You may also have to contend with lots of tiresome interruptions that will have you tearing your hair out if you let them get to you.

• *Sunday 17 November* •

An overpowering sense of restlessness threatens to take over today. The best way to handle this is to do something completely different from normal, especially if your Sundays are always the same. You'll soon feel irritable and jumpy if you're doing something that's so predictable you could do it in your sleep. If there's no escape from today's activities, at least let off steam once your time is your own otherwise you'll feel as though you're going to blow a gasket.

• *Monday 18 November* •

Try to monitor your intake of food and drink today, especially if certain items don't do you many favours at the best of times. You'll be even more susceptible to their ill effects right now. You should also be wary of swallowing medicines without good reason because these may not agree with you either. Something that will do you good is to take life easy and not stretch yourself too far.

• *Tuesday 19 November* •

Keep in touch with members of the family over the next few weeks. If you won't be seeing them during the forthcoming festivities, it's even more important to make contact with them now. Maybe you could organize a family gathering that brings everyone together, or arrange to see far-flung members of the clan in early 2003 if there's no chance of meeting up before then.

• *Wednesday 20 November* •

When you listen to the news or you read the paper, do you ever get steamed up about something and want to make your voice heard? Well, over the next couple of weeks you may well discover a cause or injustice that affects you so deeply that you can't simply shrug it off. You'll want to take action, such as joining a pressure group, writing to your MP or council, or doing something else that gets across your point of view. This may even be a turning point in your life!

• *Thursday 21 November* •

Has someone been distant or out of touch recently? If they've been physically or mentally remote, things will start to improve from today. You'll get the chance to build bridges between you once more, especially if you're prepared to talk about what happened. Even if this person couldn't help being away from you, it will still help to tell them how the separation affected you, and you'll want to know what they thought of it as well.

• *Friday 22 November* •

It's important for you to spend lots of time with people you know well during the next four weeks. There will be occasions when you feel slightly wary of the prospect of meeting strangers and you may even be overcome by attacks of shyness. This will also be a nostalgic period for you, so how about doing something positive with these sentimental feelings? For instance, if all your photos live higgledy-piggledy in carrier bags, why not give them a permanent home in some photo albums?

• *Saturday 23 November* •

Recently your routine has been starting to pall and there have been times when it's really made you angry. But today you're ready, willing and able to do something constructive about it. Whichever decisions you reach, you're determined to make them adventurous and challenging. You're no longer prepared to stick with the status quo if you can't see any good reason for it. So ring some changes and have some fun!

• *Sunday 24 November* •

It's very easy to understand how loved ones are feeling right now. It's as though you can see straight into their brains and read their minds. This is bound to make the atmosphere very amenable and easy-going because you want to keep them happy whenever possible. When you're with people you know inside out you may even find that there's little need for words because you're so attuned to one another.

• *Monday 25 November* •

You thoroughly enjoy your home comforts today, so grab every chance you can to relax within your own four walls. If you've got the time to spare, you might enjoy starting your festive preparations. Maybe you could bake the Christmas cake or cook some other goodies that you can store in the freezer until the big day? If you haven't thought about Christmas presents, start making that list now.

• *Tuesday 26 November* •

You're filled with inner confidence and contentment today. It's certainly a wonderful day for counting your blessings, and you'll run out of fingers long before you run out of reasons to be cheerful. If you pass someone who's collecting money for charity, it will be almost impossible to resist giving them some loose change. You might even be inspired to give them a note, or to make some regular contributions.

• *Wednesday 27 November* •

Domestic tension gets to you today. Certain people are easily flustered and put on the defensive, and the result will either be a strained silence or a deafening row. Try not to contribute to the stressful atmosphere by getting on your high horse too or feeling snubbed over things you'd usually shrug off. Are the difficulties you're facing really that important or is something else the cause of all this rancour?

• *Thursday 28 November* •

Things still haven't sorted themselves out at home, and once again you feel you're tiptoeing around trying to preserve everyone's finer feelings. If you managed to get through yesterday without losing your temper, don't expect to be so lucky today. It will probably be something really petty that comes as the final straw. Actually, it will probably help if you can let off steam because that will clear the air and allow things to get back to normal.

• *Friday 29 November* •

You can heave a huge sigh of relief because peace has finally broken out at home again. You may even be able to laugh at the stresses of the past few days, which will soon help to break the ice. If you're visiting the shops today you'll enjoy seeing what you can find to make your home more comfy or cosy. You might even be inspired to buy some new Christmas decorations if your current ones are looking a little worse for wear.

• *Saturday 30 November* •

The past few days haven't exactly been a picnic on the home front and you're now curious to know what sparked off the whole problem in the first place. Perhaps you should do some careful thinking on your own or maybe it would be better to have a heart-to-heart with someone you trust. Watch out, though, for a tendency to let things go round and round in your mind until you can't switch off and think about anything else.

DECEMBER AT A GLANCE

Love	♥ ♥
Money	£ $
Career	💻 💻 💻 💻
Health	☼ ☼ ☼ ☼

• *Sunday 1 December* •

The start of December finds you in a nostalgic mood. You'll really enjoy gathering your nearest and dearest around you, especially if plenty of food and drink feature at some point. It's also a nice day for doing your Christmas cards or writing lots of letters to people who live far away. A member of the family may need your help or encouragement, in which case you'll do what you can to cheer them up.

• *Monday 2 December* •

Trying to keep track of your thoughts is as easy as chasing thistledown today. You'll think about something one minute and then be left wondering what on earth it was as the entire thing vanishes from your memory banks. You'll fare much better when it comes to using your intuition and backing your hunches. If you're expected to do something complicated today, try to doublecheck it tomorrow in case you've made some howlers.

• *Tuesday 3 December* •

Whatever you have planned for today is likely to go awry at some point. This won't be through any fault of your own, it's just one of those things. If you've arranged a meeting at work, someone may turn up late or not at all, or they might make a suggestion that creates havoc. You may also have to deal with someone who seems to take a perverse delight in being as difficult and obstructive as possible.

• *Wednesday 4 December* •

Family matters are high on your list of priorities during the next few weeks, thanks to today's Totally Eclipsed New Moon. This is a very important time to get domestic projects off the ground, especially if they'll be leading to a new way of life for you. You might also welcome a new face into the family circle over the next few weeks, or realize that one chapter in your life has finally come to an end and it's time to lay some ghosts to rest.

• *Thursday 5 December* •

There's a lot going on today and life will ensure that you're kept on your toes. If you expect the unexpected you won't be disappointed because anything could happen now. You might hear from someone who's been a stranger for too long or there could be a surprise visitor. Your working life may also be subject to some unexpected developments and some changes that you weren't prepared for.

• *Friday 6 December* •

It will be horribly easy to lose confidence in yourself today, especially if you suspect that a certain someone is just waiting for you to mess up. But there is a vast gap now between reality and your version of it, and you may be taking a much more pessimistic view of things than is really necessary. If you're desperately trying to meet a deadline, you'll find it easy to concentrate and get the work done but you'll probably feel very tired at the end of it.

• *Saturday 7 December* •

It's time to have some fun! Today you need to do something that's enjoyable, entertaining and which allows you to express your true self. It doesn't have to be very serious or intellectual, and even making some Christmas decorations with the children will put a smile back on your face. If you fancy a mini treat, how about renting a video and ordering a takeaway so you can have a relaxing evening?

• *Sunday 8 December* •

If you're a typical Virgo you're no slouch when it comes to using your brain, and you're determined to remind everyone of that during the rest of December. You'll thoroughly enjoy putting your mind through its paces. For instance, you might tackle a festive competition that offers big prizes or beat everyone hands down in the pub quiz. It's also a good time to curl up with a fascinating book that you simply can't put down, especially if it involves a mystery.

• *Monday 9 December* •

You're in the mood to make some changes today and your first thought is to improve the situation at home. This might mean sorting out the kitchen cupboards and throwing away anything that will never see its sell-by date again, or it might involve thrashing out a problem that's been bothering you recently by talking it through with the people concerned. If you're fed up with your current home, you may even realize that the only answer is to move.

• *Tuesday 10 December* •

Do you want to give yourself a treat? Then make the most of your home comforts today. Even simple and inexpensive pleasures will brighten your day, so don't think that you have to spend a fortune. Of course, you may well decide to splash some cash about but that's another story! You'll enjoy pottering about in the kitchen, and you may even feel inspired enough to cook someone's favourite meal or start the festive preparations.

• *Wednesday 11 December* •

If a problem has been simmering below the surface it will erupt like a volcano today. Although this will be unpleasant and disruptive at the time, it will give you the chance to get things out into the open so you can deal with them properly. If you're the one who's got steam coming out of your ears, make sure you deal with the facts. Don't be sidetracked by past resentments that have nothing to do with the current situation.

• *Thursday 12 December* •

Are you starting to panic about all the work you've got to do before you can knock off for the holidays? Then take a deep breath and draw up a list of everything that you still have to achieve. This may take some courage, especially if you're appalled by the heaviness of your workload, but at least you'll know exactly what you're dealing with. It will also make you feel better when you can tick off each item as you achieve it.

• *Friday 13 December* •

It's very easy to get bogged down in detail today so you lose sight of your overall objectives. You might also get caught up in petty problems and silly squabbles that turn out to be a complete waste of time because they have so little meaning. Be very careful about mixing money and love because someone may use this as an excuse to make impossible demands or argue over every single penny. Life's too short . . .

• *Saturday 14 December* •

Written your Christmas cards yet? Then get cracking today while you're in the mood. Put on some festive music or your favourite CD, and just get on with it. Your brain is working extra fast today so you'll zip through everything in no time at all. This is also a marvellous day to fight your corner – not that you'll need to do any fighting. You'll be persuasive and articulate enough to get your point across without any need to jump up and down and raise your voice.

• *Sunday 15 December* •

Take things easy today because your energy is at a low ebb and your confidence is trailing around your ankles. This may well have something to do with the dispiriting atmosphere that surrounds you or the way a certain person seems determined to undermine you. But will you allow this to get you down? Yes, unfortunately! Your best bet is to keep away from troublesome people and situations whenever possible, in an act of self-preservation.

• *Monday 16 December* •

You're feeling so much more confident today that you're wondering what on earth was going on yesterday. You're also very sure of your standing in your career and long-term prospects. Throughout the year you've been considering making some changes to your current job and your daily routine, and this is a marvellous chance to start putting all your plans into action. You'll be able to combine the old and the new in ways that will lead to tremendous success and personal satisfaction.

• *Tuesday 17 December* •

If you've been working round the clock recently, it will start to catch up with you today. You're feeling tired and lethargic, and you may also feel that everything is too much effort. This means you're in need of a breather, so try to do something that won't hold up the work but will allow you to have a bit of a rest. Not even you can slog away day after day with no let-up, despite what certain people may be telling you.

• *Wednesday 18 December* •

Have you made any New Year resolutions yet? If not, this is the perfect chance to get out your 2003 diary (or buy one if you don't yet own one!) and start scribbling down your objectives. You won't want to muck about with trivial items either – you're looking for big changes because you want 2003 to be a landmark year. But don't wait until 1 January to start these resolutions – why not launch some of them straight away?

• *Thursday 19 December* •

How's that deadline coming along? If the very thought strikes dread in your heart, don't worry. Today's Full Moon is actually trying to help you to meet your targets because it's encouraging you to complete projects and will also ensure that you receive the acclaim you deserve. Over the next couple of weeks it's a good idea to look back on what you've achieved this year and to give yourself a big pat on the back.

• *Friday 20 December* •

If you're going to a seasonal party today you'll be determined to have as good a time as possible! If anyone's wearing a paper hat or blowing streamers, it will be you. After all, 'tis the season to be jolly! If you've had your eye on a certain person for some time now, you may get up Dutch courage to ask them out. What have you got to lose? But you may not want to wear your paper hat while you're doing it!

• *Saturday 21 December* •

As a Virgo you have the reputation for being a bit critical sometimes, and unfortunately this is one of those days when you're in danger of living up to it. You don't have a lot of patience right now and it shows! Try to think twice before biting someone's head off or making it plain that you think they're a blithering idiot. They're probably just as worn out and stressed as you, so take pity on them.

• *Sunday 22 December* •

Just when you were starting to flag, the planets come to the rescue! Over the next four weeks you're going to be the life and soul of the party. Your spirits are starting to rise, you're feeling far more positive than you've done recently and you're also about to receive a massive dose of self-confidence. This is exactly what you need if you're hoping to be a big hit at all those Christmas and New Year parties. Have you got the outfit to go with your infectious personality or do you need to nip out to the shops? That's what I thought . . .

• *Monday 23 December* •

You're feeling bouncy, smiley and generally on top of the world today. Even if life has kicked you on the shins in the past few days you're now determined to rise above it and find the silver lining in that cloud. No wonder people are fighting a path to your door and clamouring for your company – you're such a comforting presence! You may also have a stroke of luck that seems to come out of nowhere. Look on it as an early Christmas present!

• *Tuesday 24 December* •

It's Christmas Eve and you're full of the festive spirit. Ideally, you should be heading for the nearest party or jollification because that's exactly what you're in the mood for. But you'll try to enjoy yourself whatever you're doing now. If you're busy getting everything ready for tomorrow, try to rope in some of your loved ones and turn it into a mini celebration. You may be working but you can still have fun!

• *Wednesday 25 December* •

You're all set for a very merry Christmas! You're in a very jovial mood and you want everyone to have as good a time as possible. Your idea of heaven now is to be with some of your favourite people, eating and drinking to your heart's content. You'll enjoy playing games or romping around with the children. But you'll also appreciate having some time to yourself, so try to sneak away at some point for some much-needed peace. Ah, that's better!

• *Thursday 26 December* •

You're still in festive mood and you don't want the fun to stop yet. You're interested in any form of entertainment today, whether you're enjoying someone else's talents or you're the one who's doing the performing. If you're at home with the family, you'll like the idea of taking part in some games or charades. And if you've got tickets for the local pantomime you'll throw yourself into the spirit of the thing.

• *Friday 27 December* •

All the excitement of the past few days is starting to get to certain people, so stand by for a few tantrums and arguments. Maybe you've all been cooped up together for too long and what you need is some fresh air and a change of scene? You may also have to deal with children who are squabbling because they're jealous of each other's Christmas presents, and you've got to act as referee. It will help if you can get them all out into the great outdoors, working off their excess energy.

• *Saturday 28 December* •

The lure of the sales is starting to get to you. You can hear their siren call even if you'd promised yourself you'd stay away from them this year. Well, maybe it wouldn't hurt just to take a look . . . At least you've got the energy needed to fight your way through the crowds and it will be worth it when you snap up some bargains. If you're worried about all the calories you've consumed in the past few days, head for the gym or go for a brisk walk. And hide those chocolates in the garden shed!

• *Sunday 29 December* •

If you weren't able to be with certain people during the recent festivities, they're on your list of must-sees now. You'll really enjoy doing the rounds, dropping in on chums and catching up on all the gossip. Love will also brighten up your life today. You might have a lovely time with your other half or you may meet someone new who makes your knees go all wobbly and your heart pound faster than the Minute Waltz.

• *Monday 30 December* •

You really are having a wonderful time at the moment and this is another day when it's enjoyment all the way. You'll especially enjoy getting together with some neighbours or close relatives and raising a glass to the season. In fact, if you haven't exactly been chummy with a certain someone recently, this is a marvellous chance to bury the hatchet and start anew. You can't see the point in keeping old feuds going for longer than necessary.

• *Tuesday 31 December* •

It's the last day of the year and you want to celebrate in style. But you may be more interested in a cosy night at home with your loved ones than being part of a throng of people in public. You're very appreciative of your home comforts today, and you may also be feeling rather sentimental. How about curling up on the sofa with that special someone and your favourite film? Right now, you can't think of anything nicer. Happy new year!

YOUR VIRGO SUN SIGN

In this chapter I am going to tell you all about your Virgo Sun sign. But what is a Sun sign? It often gets called a star sign, but are they the same thing? Well, yes, although 'Sun sign' is a more accurate term. Your Sun sign is the sign that the Sun occupied when you were born. Every year, the Sun moves through the heavens and spends an average of 30 days in each of the twelve signs. When you were born, the Sun was moving through the sign of Virgo, so this is your Sun or star sign.

This chapter tells you everything you want to know about your Sun sign. To start off, I describe your general personality – what makes you tick. Then I talk about your attitude to relationships, the way you handle money, what your Sun sign says about your health and, finally, which careers are best for you. Put all that together and you will have a well-rounded picture of yourself.

Character

If there were a prize for being methodical, efficient, practical and modest (despite this list of virtues), you would win it hands down. No one else would even come close. It's one of your greatest strengths and also one of your biggest curses. It's a strength because it makes you so reliable. It's a curse because this reliability is often exploited by others or taken for granted. And your need to be of service to other people means that you often do things that are above and beyond the call of duty. You feel that you'll be letting yourself and them down if you do any less.

At the risk of embarrassing you (always a danger with Virgos), you are the unsung hero or heroine of the zodiac. The world would come to a grinding halt without Virgos making sure that everything is ticking over nicely, yet somehow you rarely receive the applause you deserve. Your innate modesty, and your tendency to retreat from the limelight, prevent you elbowing other people aside and grabbing the glory you deserve.

If you're a typical Virgo you're very astute and very sharp. No one can pull the wool over your eyes because you've already smelt a rat and are watching to see what will happen next. You also have a highly developed critical sense. It enables you to spot the difference between deceit and truth, gold and dross. It also makes you extremely tough on yourself because you always think you could do so much better if you only tried harder. Yet your idea of being second-rate is often everyone else's example of exemplary behaviour. Maybe you should let yourself off the hook every now and then?

Relationships

This is often a difficult area for you. And to prove it, there are more single and/or celibate Virgos in the world than any other sign. Your high standards tell you that if you can't be with someone very special, you'd rather not be with anyone at all, thank you very much. You don't want to settle for second best. Relationships can also be difficult for you because it's sometimes hard for you to express your emotions. You tend to clam up and may even think there's something rather embarrassing about open demonstrations of affection. It may take a lot of love and patience from other people to make you change your mind. This is especially likely if you grew up in a family where affection was displayed only on special occasions. Sex, however, is another matter! Many Virgos have a very red-blooded approach to sex, which is definitely encouraged by the Earth element to which you belong.

Your ruling planet, Mercury, gives you a tremendous respect for intelligence. Even if you meet someone who's so attractive that they belong on the cover of a magazine, you won't be interested in a long-term relationship if they're as stupid as a fence post. You've got better things to do with your time!

You are very critical of yourself and sometimes this spills over into criticism of your loved ones. You may think you're doing them a favour by pointing out their flaws, but they may see it as one long nagging session in which they can't do anything right. So try to temper your criticisms with some praise every now and then.

Money

This is an area where you really come into your own. You have a natural empathy for money and what it can buy, so you usually manage your own finances very well. If you do lose track of what's going on in your bank account, it's probably because you're going through some sort of crisis. But it's a rare Virgo who makes the same mistakes twice.

Even if your career doesn't involve handling money, you may find yourself acting as an unofficial financial adviser to people. Something may tell them that you'll know the best credit card deals or which bank is best for small businesses.

When it comes to spending money, you're not always over-generous. There are usually very good reasons for this (such as being unable to afford it), but sometimes it's because of a careful attitude towards money that verges on the penny-pinching. You're especially reluctant to spend money on yourself, even if you lavish it on your children or partner. Perhaps you think you don't deserve it?

Health

We're on home ground here! Your sign has a very powerful affinity with all aspects of health, from worrying about it to treating people when they're ill. Even if you don't work with health in some way, you are probably extremely interested in the subject. You may subscribe to a health magazine or read lots of books on health, especially if they're on the subject of complementary health.

It has to be said that Virgos are often confirmed hypochondriacs! No sooner have you read about an ailment than you start to imagine that you've got it. You may also interpret every twinge and ache in the worst possible light, thinking you've got all sorts of terrible diseases. Very often the worst thing you suffer from is worry and anxiety, which can play havoc with your body and make you feel pretty wretched. You can also suffer from stomach and digestive problems. Such embarrassing ailments as irritable bowel syndrome are especially prevalent among Virgos.

You place tremendous importance on eating a healthy diet, even if that means you're the only one in your family who eats your greens. Organic food or a vegetarian or vegan diet may appeal to you, and you may even have a food allergy that requires a special diet. When looking for treatments for your health problems, complementary therapies may sometimes be most suitable for your delicate nervous system.

Career

It may be a truism, but when it comes to work you definitely believe in service with a smile. You have such a strong urge to be of service to others that it can even work against you, because you'll put in more hours than everyone else and be much more conscientious than your colleagues.

Among the careers that suit you are anything to do with accountancy, agency work, secretarial work, the medical profession, veterinary work and religion. You're a whizz at running an office and making sure everyone is doing what they're meant to. You enjoy setting up systems to make everything run more efficiently, and will try to take advantage of the latest technology to keep track of phone calls, e-mails and other forms of communication.

You like turning your colleagues into your friends, although you may find it difficult to overcome your reservations if you're working with someone who isn't very bright. Somehow you'll never manage to forget it!

You are ultra-dependable, so your bosses and colleagues always know they can count on you in a crisis. You'll work round the clock if necessary, but try not to get into a situation where you're the only one who does this while everyone else enjoys their eight hours of sleep each night. Although it might be a different story, of course, if you're receiving lavish amounts of overtime pay!

LOVE AND THE STARS

Have you ever wondered why you get on so well with some signs and never seem to hit it off with others? Do you send out stacks of birthday cards at particular times of the year because you know so many people born under those signs, while you don't know anyone who's born at other times of the year? Have you ever wondered why this is? Well, astrology has the answers!

If you're fed up with your relationships being like a lottery, because you aren't sure if you'll hit the jackpot or end up with nothing, this guide will give you some astrological help in getting on well with the people around you. It's arranged sign by sign, with your own sign heading the list. I describe how you get on with each sign – what brings you together or perhaps what can drive you apart. Once you've read about how your sign gets on with the other members of the zodiac, you can read what the other signs think of you! Turn to the sign of your friend or your partner and find out how they get along with you. You might gain some very interesting insights into how your relationship works. Do you get on like a house on fire, or is it more like fireworks when you get together?

At the end of my astrological guide to love, there are two

compatibility charts so you can see at a glance how you get on with all the Sun signs, as lovers and also as friends. Each combination has been marked out of ten, so you can see whether you're soulmates or your relationship requires lots of work. Ten means it's everything you ever wanted while one means that you feel like asking for your money back. Having said that, don't panic if your current relationship gets a low score. Every Sun sign combination has the potential to be a success, but some are easier to deal with than others.

All you need to do is look for the woman's Sun sign along the top of the chart and then find the man's sign down the side. The box where the two meet will show how well they get on together.

Virgo

As you might imagine, Virgos are happy with their fellow Earth signs of Taurus and Capricorn because they share the same practical attitude. A Virgo enjoys the steady, reassuring company of a Taurean, and they might even learn to relax a little instead of worrying themselves into the ground over the slightest problem. When two Virgos get together it can be too much of a good thing. Although at first they'll love talking to someone who shares so many of their preoccupations and ideas, they can soon drive one another round the bend. When a Virgo first meets a Capricorn they're delighted to know someone who's obviously got their head screwed on. It's only later on that they wish the Capricorn could lighten up every now and then.

Virgos get on well with Cancerians, Scorpios and Pisceans, the three Water signs. A Virgo enjoys being looked after by a considerate Cancerian, although they'll worry about their waistline and may get irritated by the Cancerian's super-sensitive feelings. You can expect plenty of long, analytical conversations when a Virgo gets together with a Scorpio. They both love getting to the bottom of subjects and will endlessly talk things through. They'll also get on extremely well in the bedroom. Pisces is Virgo's opposite sign, but although some opposites thrive in each other's company, that isn't always the case with this combination. The Virgo could soon grow impatient with the dreamy Piscean and will long to tell them a few home truths.

Although the other Earth signs don't usually get on well with Air signs, it's different for Virgos. They understand the intellectual energies of Geminis, Librans and Aquarians. A Virgo thrives in a Gemini's company, and they spend hours chatting over the phone if they can't get together in person. It's difficult for them to discuss their emotions, however, and they may never tell each other how they really feel. A Virgo admires a sophisticated, charming Libran, and marvels at their diplomacy. How do they do it? Expect a few sparks to fly when a Virgo pairs up with an Aquarian, because both of them have very strong opinions and aren't afraid to air them. The result is a lot of hot air and some vigorous arguments.

The three Fire signs – Aries, Leo and Sagittarius – are a source of endless fascination to a Virgo. They've got so much energy! A Virgo finds an Arien exciting but their relationship could be short-lived because the Virgo will be so irritated by the Arien's devil-may-care attitude to life. When a Virgo pairs up with a Leo, they'll be intrigued by this person's comparatively lavish lifestyle but their own modest temperament will be shocked if the Leo enjoys showing off. A Virgo is able to talk to a Sagittarius until the cows come home – they're both fascinated by ideas, although the precise Virgo will first be amused, and then irritated, by the Sagittarian's rather relaxed attitude to hard facts.

Libra

Of all the members of the zodiac, this is the one that finds it easiest to get on with the other signs. Librans get on particularly well with Geminis and Aquarians, their fellow Air signs. A Libran is enchanted by a Gemini's quick brain and ready wit, and they enjoy endless discussions on all sorts of subjects. When two Librans get together, they revel in the resulting harmonious atmosphere but it's almost impossible for them to reach any decisions – each one defers to the other while being unable to say what they really want. A Libran is intrigued by the independence and sharp mind of an Aquarian, but their feelings could be hurt by the Aquarian's emotional coolness.

Libra enjoys being with the three Fire signs – Aries, Leo and Sagittarius. Libra, who often takes life at rather a slow pace, is energized by a lively Arien, and they complement one another's personalities well. However, the LIbran may occasionally feel hurt by the Arien's single-mindedness and blunt speech. A Libran adores the luxury-loving ways of a Leo, and they'll both spend a fortune in the pursuit of happiness. They also get on well in the bedroom. When a Libran gets together with an exuberant Sagittarian, they'll have great fun. All the same, the Sagittarian need for honesty could fluster the Libran, who adopts a much more diplomatic approach to life.

Although the other two Air signs can find it hard to understand members of the Water element, it's different for Librans. They're more sympathetic to the emotional energies of Cancerians, Scorpios and Pisceans. A Libran delights in the protective care of a Cancerian, but those ever-changing Cancerian moods may be hard for a balanced Libran to take. Those deep Scorpio emotions will intrigue the Libran but they may quickly become bogged down by such an intense outlook on life and will be desperate for some light relief. As for Pisces, the Libran is charmed by the Piscean's delicate nature and creative gifts, but both signs hate facing up to unpleasant facts so this couple may never deal with any problems that lie between them.

Libra enjoys the reliable natures of Taurus, Virgo and Capricorn, the Earth signs. A Libran appreciates the company of a relaxed and easy-going Taurean, although they may sometimes regret the Taurean's lack of imagination. When a Libran and a Virgo get together, the Libran enjoys the Virgo's mental abilities but their critical comments will soon cut the Libran to the quick. The Libran may not come back for a second tongue-lashing. A Libran understands the ambitions of a Capricorn, and likes their steady nature and the way they support their family. However, there could soon be rows about money, with the Libran spending a lot more than the Capricorn thinks is necessary.

Scorpio

Not every sign gets on well with its fellow members, yet an astonishing number of Scorpios pair up. They feel safe together because they know the worst and best about each other. When things are good, they're brilliant but these two can also bring out the worst in each other, with intense silences and brooding sulks. A Scorpio enjoys the tender ministrations of a loving Cancerian, and adores being with someone who's so obviously concerned about their welfare. Feelings run deep when a Scorpio pairs up with a Piscean, although the Scorpio may become impatient with the Piscean's reluctance to face up to unpalatable truths.

The three Earth signs – Taurus, Virgo and Capricorn – are well suited to the Scorpio temperament. Those astrological opposites, Scorpio and Taurus, enjoy a powerful relationship, much of which probably takes place in the bedroom, but whenever they have a disagreement there's an atmosphere you could cut with a knife, and neither of them will be prepared to admit they were in the wrong. A Scorpio is attracted to a neat, analytical Virgo but their feelings will be hurt by this sign's tendency to criticize. What's more, their pride stops them telling the Virgo how they feel. The Scorpio admires a practical Capricorn, especially if they've earned a lot of respect through their work, but this could be a rather chilly pairing because both signs find it difficult to show their feelings.

When you put a Scorpio together with one of the three Fire signs, they'll either get on famously or won't understand one another at all. A Scorpio revels in the lusty Arien's sex drive, although they'll soon feel tired if they try to keep up with the Arien's busy schedule. The combination of Scorpio and Leo packs quite a punch. They're both very strong personalities, but they boss one another around like mad and find it almost impossible to achieve a compromise if they fall out. A Scorpio likes to take life at a measured pace, so they're bemused by a Sagittarian's need to keep busy all the time. In the end, they'll become fed up with never seeing the Sagittarian, or playing second fiddle to all their other interests.

Scorpio is bemused by the three Air signs – Gemini, Libra and Aquarius – because they operate on such completely different wavelengths. A Scorpio can be good friends with a Gemini but they're at emotional cross-purposes, with the Scorpio's intense approach to life too much for a light-hearted Gemini to cope with. Emotions are also the bugbear between a Scorpio and a Libran. Everything is great at first, but the Scorpio's powerful feelings and dark moods will eventually send the Libran running in the opposite direction. You can expect some tense arguments when a Scorpio pairs up with an Aquarian – they're both convinced that they're right and the other one is wrong.

Sagittarius

When a Sagittarian pairs up with a fellow Fire sign, there's plenty of warmth and the odd firework. A Sagittarian is thrilled by the adventurous spirit of an Arien, and they love exploring the world together. There are plenty of tall tales when a Sagittarian gets together with a Leo – they'll try to outdo each other, dropping names and recounting their greatest triumphs. If the Leo is slightly pompous, the Sagittarian is able to take them down a peg or two, but they must beware of hurting the Leo's feelings. As for two Sagittarians, they'll spur each other on and encourage one another to gain as much experience of life as possible. You probably won't be able to move in their house for books.

With their endless curiosity about the world, Sagittarians understand the intellectual Air signs very well. A Sagittarian enjoys the chatty company of a Gemini and, because they're opposite numbers in the zodiac, the Sagittarian is able to encourage the Gemini to see things through and explore them in more detail than usual. A refined and diplomatic Libran will try to teach the blunt Sagittarian not to say the first thing that pops into their head. However, the Sagittarian may eventually find the Libran's sense of balance rather trying – why can't they get more worked up about things? There's plenty of straight talking when a Sagittarian teams up with an Aquarian – they both have a high regard for honesty. The independent Sagittarian respects the Aquarian's need for freedom, but may feel rather stung by their periods of emotional coolness.

A Sagittarian will struggle to understand the Earth signs. They respect the Taurean's ability to work hard but they're driven to distraction by their reluctance to make changes and break out of any ruts they've fallen into. A Sagittarian enjoys talking to a brainy Virgo, but their expansive and spontaneous nature could eventually be restricted by the Virgo's need to think things through before taking action. When a Sagittarian gets together with a Capricorn, it's a case of optimism versus pessimism. While the Sagittarian's glass is half-full, the Capricorn's is always half-empty, and this causes many rows and possibly some ill feeling.

There could be lots of misunderstandings when a Sagittarian gets involved with one of the Water signs. A Sagittarian needs a bigger social circle than their family, whereas a Cancerian is quite happy surrounded by kith and kin. The Sagittarian need for independence won't go down well, either. It's like oil and water when a Sagittarian pairs up with a Scorpio. The Sagittarian is the roamer of the zodiac, whereas the Scorpio wants them where they can see them, in case they're up to no good. All will be well if the Sagittarian gets together with a strong-minded Piscean. In fact, they'll really enjoy one another's company. A Piscean who's lost in a world of their own, however, will soon leave them cold.

Capricorn

Despite their outward poise, a Capricorn is very easily hurt so they need to know their feelings won't be trampled on. There's least danger of that when they get together with a fellow Earth sign. A Capricorn adores a Taurean's deep sense of responsibility and they'll both work hard to create their ideal home. A Capricorn appreciates the methodical approach of a Virgo, but could feel deeply hurt by the Virgo's sharp tongue and caustic remarks. If two Capricorns team up, one of them must be demonstrative and openly affectionate, otherwise the relationship could be rather sterile and serious.

Capricorns also feel safe with members of the Water signs.

When a Capricorn gets together with a Cancerian, they do their utmost to make their home a haven. They'll get great satisfaction from channelling their energies into bringing up a family. A Capricorn may be rather bemused by the depth and intensity of a Scorpio's emotions – Capricorns are too reserved to indulge in such drama themselves and it can make them feel uncomfortable. A no-nonsense Capricorn could be perplexed by an extremely vulnerable Piscean and won't know how to handle them. Should they give them a hanky or tell them to pull themselves together?

The Air signs can also make a Capricorn feel somewhat unsettled. They're fascinated by a Gemini's breadth of knowledge and endless chat, but they also find them superficial and rather flighty. In fact, the Capricorn probably doesn't trust the Gemini. A Capricorn feels far happier in the company of a Libran. Here's someone who seems much steadier emotionally and who can help the Capricorn to unwind after a hard day's work. It can be great or ghastly when a Capricorn sets their sights on an Aquarian. They understand each other provided the Aquarian isn't too unconventional, but the Capricorn feels uncomfortable and embarrassed by any displays of eccentricity, deliberate or not.

The Fire signs help to warm up the Capricorn, who can be rather remote and distant at times. A Capricorn admires the Arien's drive and initiative, but endlessly tells them to look before they leap and could become irritated when they don't take this sage advice. When a Capricorn gets together with a Leo, they won't need to worry about appearances – the Capricorn will feel justly proud of the smart Leo. However, they could wince when the bills come in and they discover how much those clothes cost. A Capricorn thinks a Sagittarian must have come from another planet – how can they be so relaxed and laid-back all the time? They have great respect for the Sagittarian's wisdom and philosophy, but they quickly become fed up with having to fit in around the Sagittarian's hectic social life.

Aquarius

Put an Aquarian with a fellow Air sign and they're happy. They thoroughly enjoy being with a lively Gemini and love discussing everything under the sun with them. They may not have a very exciting sex life, but their mental closeness will more than make up for it. The gentle charm of a Libran calms down an Aquarian when their nerves become frayed, although they disapprove of the Libran's innate tact and diplomacy – why can't they just say what they think, instead of sitting on the fence? With two Aquarians you never know what to expect, other than that they'll be great friends. They'll certainly do a lot of talking, but could spend more time debating esoteric ideas and abstract concepts.

An Aquarian likes all the Fire signs, although they find Ariens hard to fathom and can become exhausted by an Arien's endless supply of energy and enthusiasm. There are no such problems when an Aquarian pairs up with a Leo because they complement each other in many ways. The Aquarian teaches objectivity to the Leo, who in return encourages the Aquarian to express their emotions more. An Aquarian thoroughly enjoys being with a Sagittarian because both of them hate being tied down. As a result, they respect one another's independence and will probably rarely see each other because of all their spare-time activities.

It's not quite so simple when an Aquarian joins forces with one of the Earth signs. An Aquarian will lock horns with a Taurean sooner or later, because neither of them is able to back down once a disagreement has started. The Aquarian will also feel very restricted by the Taurean's possessiveness. The Virgo's analytical approach to life intrigues the Aquarian but they'll sit up all night arguing the toss over everything, with each one convinced that they've got all the answers. When an Aquarian meets a Capricorn, they've got their work cut out for them if they're to find a happy medium between the erratic Aquarian and the conventional Capricorn.

An Aquarian feels out of their depth when they're with one of the Water signs. They simply don't understand what makes a Cancerian tick – why do they worry themselves sick over things that they can't change? The Aquarian finds it all most peculiar. They also find it difficult to understand a Scorpio who takes so many things so seriously. Although the Aquarian also has a list of topics that mean a lot to them, they're not the sort of things that hold the slightest interest for a Scorpio. It's more or less the same story with a Pisces, because their huge resources of emotion make the Aquarian feel uncomfortable and fill them with a strong desire to escape as fast as possible.

Pisces

Relationships mean a lot to a sensitive Piscean, but they're easily misunderstood by many of the more robust signs. There are no such worries with the other Water signs, however. A Piscean loves being with a tender Cancerian who knows how to help them relax and feel safe. They really enjoy playing house together but the emotional scenes will blow the roof off. The relationship between a Piscean and a Scorpio can be quite spicy and sexy, but the Piscean is turned off if the Scorpio becomes too intense and dramatic. Two Pisceans feel safe with one another, but they'll push all their problems under the carpet unless one of them is more objective.

A Piscean also gets on well with the Earth signs, although with a few reservations. A Piscean takes comfort from being looked after by a protective Taurean, but after a while they could feel stifled by the Taurean's possessive and matter-of-fact attitude. The relationship between a Piscean and a Virgo starts off well but the Piscean could soon feel crushed by the

Virgo's criticism and will need more emotional reassurance than the Virgo is able to give. A Piscean feels safe with a Capricorn because they're so dependable but in the end this may begin to bug them. It's not that they want the Capricorn to two-time them, more that they'd like a little unpredictability every now and then.

A Piscean is fascinated by the Air signs but their apparent lack of emotion could cause problems. A Piscean and a Gemini are terrific friends but could encounter difficulties as lovers. The Piscean's strong emotional needs are too much for the Gemini to handle – they'll feel as if they're drowning. The Piscean is on much firmer ground with a Libran, who'll go out of their way to keep the Piscean happy. Neither sign is good at facing up to any nasty truths, however. An Aquarian is too much for a sensitive Piscean, who views the world through rose-coloured specs. An Aquarian, on the other hand, has uncomfortably clear vision.

The Fire signs can cheer up a Piscean enormously, but any prolonged displays of emotion will make the Fire signs feel weighed down. The Piscean is fascinated by an Arien's exploits but could feel reluctant to join in. They'll also be easily hurt by some of the Arien's off-the-cuff remarks. When a Piscean pairs up with a Leo they appreciate the way the Leo wants to take charge and look after them. After a while, however, this could grate on them and they'll want to be more independent. A Piscean enjoys discussing philosophy and spiritual ideas with a Sagittarian – they can sit up half the night talking things through. The Sagittarian brand of honesty could hurt the Piscean at times, but they know this isn't malicious and will quickly forgive such outbursts.

Aries

Because Ariens belong to the Fire element, they get on very well with their fellow Fire signs Leo and Sagittarius. All the same, an Arien getting together with a Leo will soon notice a distinct drop in their bank balance, because they'll enjoy going to all the swankiest restaurants and sitting in the best seats at the theatre. When an Arien pairs up with a Sagittarian, they'll compete over who drives the fastest car and has the most exciting holidays. When two Ariens get together the results can be combustible. Ideally, one Arien should be a lot quieter, otherwise they'll spend most of their time jostling for power. All these combinations are very sexy and physical.

Ariens also thrive in the company of the three Air signs – Gemini, Libra and Aquarius. Of the three, they get on best with Geminis, who share their rather childlike view of the world and also their sense of fun. An Arien and a Gemini enjoy hatching all sorts of ideas and schemes, even if they never get round to putting them into action. There's an exciting sense of friction between Aries and Libra, their opposite number in the zodiac. An Arien will be enchanted by the way their Libran caters to their every need, but may become impatient when the Libran also wants to look after other people. An Arien will be captivated by the originality of an Aquarian, although at times they'll be driven mad by the Aquarian's eccentric approach to life and the way they blow hot and cold in the bedroom.

Ariens don't do so well with the Earth signs – Taurus, Virgo and Capricorn. The very careful, slightly plodding nature of a typical Taurean can drive an Arien barmy at times, and although they'll respect – and benefit from – the Taurean's practical approach to life, it can still fill them with irritation. An Arien finds it difficult to fathom a Virgo, because their attitudes to life are diametrically opposed. An Arien likes to jump in with both feet, while a Virgo prefers to take things slowly and analyse every possibility before committing themselves. An Arien can get on quite well with a Capricorn, because they're linked by their sense of ambition and their earthy sexual needs.

An Arien is out of their depth with any of the Water signs – Cancer, Scorpio and Pisces. They quickly become irritated by the defensive Cancerian, although they'll love their cooking. An Arien will enjoy a very passionate affair with a Scorpio, but the Scorpio's need to know exactly what the Arien is up to when their back is turned will soon cause problems and rifts. Although an Arien may begin a relationship with a Pisces by wanting to look after them and protect them from the harsh realities of life, eventually the Piscean's extremely sensitive nature may bring out the Arien's bullying streak.

Taurus

Taureans are literally in their element when they're with Virgos or Capricorns who, like themselves, are Earth signs. Two Taureans will get along very happily together, although they could become so wedded to routine that they get stuck in a rut. They may also encourage one another to eat too much. A Taurean will enjoy being with a Virgo, because they respect the Virgo's methodical nature. They'll also like encouraging their Virgo to relax and take life easy. Money will form a link between a Taurean and a Capricorn, with plenty of serious discussions on how to make it and what to do with it once they've got it. There will also be a strong sexual rapport, and the Taurean will encourage the more sensual side of the Capricorn.

The relationship between a Taurean and members of the Water element is also very good. A Taurean and a Cancerian will revel in one another's company and will probably be so happy at home that they'll rarely stir from their armchairs. They both have a strong need for emotional security and will stick together through thick and thin. There's plenty of passion when a Taurean pairs up with a Scorpio, although the faithful Taurean could become fed up with the Scorpio's jealous nature. They simply won't understand what they're being accused of, and their loyal nature will be offended by the very thought that they could be a two-timer. A Taurean will be delighted by a delicate Piscean, and will want to take care of such a vulnerable and sensitive creature.

Things become rather more complicated when a Taurean pairs up with an Arien, Leo or Sagittarian, all of whom are Fire signs. They have very little in common – Taureans like to take things slowly while Fire signs want to make things happen *now*. It's particularly difficult between a Taurean and an Arien – the careful Taurean will feel harried and rushed by the impetuous Arien. It's a little better when a Taurean gets together with a Leo, because they share a deep appreciation of the good things in life, although the Taurean will be horrified by the Leo's ability to spend money. Making joint decisions could be difficult, however, because they'll both stand their ground and refuse to budge. A Taurean and a Sagittarian simply don't understand each other – they're on such different wavelengths. Any Taurean displays of possessiveness will make the independent Sagittarian want to run a mile.

Taureans are equally mystified by the Air signs – Gemini, Libra and Aquarius. What they see as the flightiness of Gemini drives them barmy – why can't the Gemini settle down and do one thing at a time? The Taurean will probably feel quite exhausted by the Gemini's many interests and bubbly character. Taurus and Libra are a surprisingly good pairing, because they share a need for beauty, luxury and love. This could end up costing the penny-wise Taurean quite a packet, but they'll have a deliciously romantic time along the way. Taurus and Aquarius are chalk and cheese, and neither one is prepared to meet the other one halfway. The Taurean need to keep tabs on their loved one's every movement will irritate the freedom-loving Aquarian, and there will be plenty of rows as a result.

Gemini

One of the Air signs, Geminis get on very well with their fellow members of this element – Librans and Aquarians. Two Geminis are the astrological equivalent of double trouble – they chat nineteen to the dozen and revel in the company of someone who understands them so well. A Gemini delights in being with a Libran, because they enjoy the intellectual company and will benefit from the Libran's (usually) relaxed approach to life. They'll also learn to deal with their emotions more if a sympathetic Libran can guide them. Gemini and Aquarius is a very exciting pairing – the Gemini is encouraged to think deeply and knows that the Aquarian won't put up with any woolly ideas or fudged arguments.

Geminis also get on well with the three Fire signs – Aries, Leo and Sagittarius. A Gemini loves being with a racy, adventurous Arien, and together they enjoy keeping abreast of all the latest gossip and cultural developments. However, after the first flush of enthusiasm has worn off, the Gemini may find the Arien's strong need for sex rather hard to take. The Gemini gets on very well with a Leo. They delight in the Leo's affectionate nature and are amused by their need to have the best that money can buy – and they'll gladly share in the spoils. Gemini and Sagittarius are an excellent combination, because they sit opposite each other in the zodiac and so complement one another's character. The Gemini will be fascinated by the erudite and knowledgeable Sagittarian.

Gemini doesn't do so well with the Earth signs of Taurus and Capricorn, although they get on better with Virgo. The Gemini finds it difficult to understand a Taurean, because they see the world from such different viewpoints. The Gemini takes a more light-hearted approach and lives life at such a speed that they find it difficult to slow down to the more measured pace of a Taurean. The wonderfully dry Capricorn sense of humour is a source of constant delight to a Gemini. However, they're less taken with the Capricorn's streak of pessimism and their love of tradition. Of the three Earth signs, Gemini and Virgo are the most compatible. The Gemini shares the Virgo's brain power and they have long, fascinating conversations.

When a Gemini gets together with the Water signs, the result can be enjoyable or puzzling. Gemini and Cancer have little in common, because the Gemini wants to spread their emotional and intellectual wings, whereas a Cancerian likes to stay close to home and has little interest in abstract ideas. Gemini finds Scorpio perplexing because they operate on such different levels. A Gemini tends to skim along the surface of things, so often deals with life on a superficial level, whereas a Scorpio likes to dig deep and has to have an emotional investment in everything they do. A Gemini appreciates the subtlety and sensitivity of a Piscean, but they're likely to make off-the-cuff comments that unwittingly hurt the Piscean.

Cancer

Cancerians revel in the company of their fellow Water signs of Scorpio and Pisces. When two Cancerians get together they could spend most of their time at home or eating – preferably both. They feel safe in the knowledge that they both have a strong need for love, but their innate Cancerian tenacity may mean they cling on to the relationship even if it's long past its best. A Cancerian is enchanted with a Scorpio, because at last they feel free to really let rip emotionally. However, the intuitive Cancerian should beware of soaking up the Scorpio's darker moods like a psychic sponge. A Cancerian will take one look at a delicate Piscean and want to invite them home for a good hot meal. All the Cancerian's protective instincts are aroused by a gentle Piscean, but their anger will also be aroused if it turns out the Piscean has been leading a double life behind their back.

Cancerians also find a great deal of comfort in the company of the Earth signs – Taurus, Virgo and Capricorn. Cancer and Taurus were made for each other – they both adore home comforts and they trust one another implicitly. The Cancerian loves making a cosy nest for their hard-working Taurean. A Cancerian finds a Virgo a more difficult proposition, especially emotionally. Whereas Cancer is all warm hugs and holding hands by the fire, Virgo prefers to read a book and reserve any displays of affection for the bedroom. Cancer and Capricorn are opposite numbers in the zodiac, so share a tremendous rapport. They also share the same values of home, tradition and family, and if anyone can help a Capricorn to relax and take life easy, it's a Cancerian.

Life becomes more difficult when it comes to a Cancerian's relationship with any of the Air signs. They simply don't understand one another. A Cancerian can't make a Gemini out. They feel confused by what they think of as the Gemini's flightiness and inability to stay in one place for long. They can also be easily hurt by the Gemini's difficulty in expressing their emotions. A Cancerian gets on much better with a Libran. They're both ambitious in their own ways and so have a great deal in common. The Cancerian enjoys the Libran's romantic nature, but the Cancerian tendency to cling doesn't go down well. A Cancerian regards a typical Aquarian as a being from another planet. They're hurt by the Aquarian's strong need for independence and dislike of having to account for their every action, and are dismayed and confused by the Aquarian's hot-and-cold attitude to sex.

The Fire signs of Aries, Leo and Sagittarius are also a potential source of bewilderment to the gentle Cancerian. They understand the drive and ambition of an Arien, but will be stung by their blunt speech and worried about their daredevil tendencies. What if they hurt themselves? A Cancerian gets on well with a Leo because they share a strong love of family and are both openly affectionate and loving. The Cancerian enjoys creating a home that the Leo can feel proud of. So far, so good, but the story isn't so simple when a Cancerian pairs up with a Sagittarian. They're too different to understand one another – the Cancerian wants to stay at home with the family while the Sagittarian has an instinctive need to roam the world. As a result, the Cancerian will be disappointed, and then hurt, when the Sagittarian's busy schedule takes them away from home too often.

Leo

Leos adore the company of their fellow Fire signs, Aries and Sagittarius. They understand one another and enjoy each other's spontaneous warmth and affection. A Leo is amused by the exuberance and impulsiveness of an Arien, and they enjoy being persuaded to let their hair down a bit and not worry too much about appearances. A Leo enjoys the dash and vitality of a Sagittarian, although they may feel irritated if they can never get hold of them on the phone or the Sagittarian is always off doing other things. Two Leos together either love or loathe one another. One of them should be prepared to take a back seat, otherwise they'll both be vying for the limelight all the time.

The three Air signs of Gemini, Libra and Aquarius all get on well with Leos. When a Leo pairs up with a Gemini, you can expect lots of laughter and plenty of fascinating conversations. The demonstrative Leo is able to help the Gemini be more openly affectionate and loving. Leo and Libra is a great combination, and the Leo is enchanted by the Libran's fair-minded attitude. Both signs love luxury and all the good things in life but their bank managers may not be so pleased by the amount of money they manage to spend. Leo and Aquarius sit opposite one another across the horoscope, so they already have a great deal in common. They're fascinated by one another but they're both very stubborn, so any disputes between them usually end in stalemate because neither is prepared to concede any ground.

Leos don't really understand the Earth signs. Although Leos admire their practical approach to life, they find it rather restricting. A Leo enjoys the sensuous and hedonistic side of a Taurean's character but may become frustrated by their fear of change. Leo and Virgo have very little in common, especially when it comes to food – the Leo wants to tuck in at all the best restaurants while the Virgo is worried about the state of the kitchens, the number of calories and the size of the bill. A Leo respects the Capricorn's desire to support their family and approves of their need to be seen in the best possible light, but they feel hurt by the Capricorn's difficulty in showing their feelings.

When a Leo gets together with one of the Water signs – Cancer, Scorpio or Pisces – they'll enjoy the sexual side of the relationship but could eventually feel stifled by all that Watery emotion. A Leo and a Cancerian adore making a home together and both dote on their children. The Leo also likes comforting their vulnerable Cancerian – provided this doesn't happen too often. A Leo and a Scorpio will be powerfully attracted to one another, but power could also pull them apart – who's going to wear the trousers? They'll also lock horns during rows and both of them will refuse to back down. A Leo delights in a sophisticated Piscean, but may become irritated by their indecision and jangly nerves.

Compatibility in Love and Sex at a glance

M \ F	♈	♉	♊	♋	♌	♍	♎	♏	♐	♑	♒	♓
♈	8	5	9	7	9	4	7	8	9	7	7	3
♉	6	8	4	10	7	8	8	7	3	8	2	8
♊	8	2	7	3	8	7	9	4	9	4	9	4
♋	5	10	4	8	6	5	6	8	2	9	2	8
♌	9	8	9	7	7	4	9	6	8	7	9	6
♍	4	8	6	4	4	7	6	7	7	9	4	4
♎	7	8	10	7	8	5	9	6	9	6	10	6
♏	7	9	4	7	6	6	7	10	5	6	5	7
♐	9	4	10	4	9	7	8	4	9	6	9	5
♑	7	8	4	9	6	8	6	4	4	8	4	5
♒	8	6	9	4	9	4	9	6	8	7	8	2
♓	7	6	7	9	6	7	6	9	7	5	4	9

1 = the pits
10 = the peaks

Key

♈ – Aries
♉ – Taurus
♊ – Gemini
♋ – Cancer
♌ – Leo
♍ – Virgo
♎ – Libra
♏ – Scorpio
♐ – Sagittarius
♑ – Capricorn
♒ – Aquarius
♓ – Pisces

Compatibility in Friendship at a glance

M \ F	♈	♉	♊	♋	♌	♍	♎	♏	♐	♑	♒	♓
♈	8	5	10	5	9	3	7	8	9	6	8	5
♉	6	9	6	10	7	8	7	6	4	9	3	9
♊	9	3	9	4	9	8	10	5	10	5	10	6
♋	6	9	4	9	5	4	6	9	4	10	3	9
♌	10	7	9	6	9	4	8	6	9	6	9	7
♍	5	9	8	4	4	8	5	8	8	10	5	6
♎	8	9	10	8	8	6	9	5	9	6	10	7
♏	7	8	5	8	7	7	6	9	4	5	6	8
♐	9	5	10	4	10	8	8	4	10	7	9	6
♑	6	9	5	10	6	9	5	5	4	9	5	6
♒	9	6	10	5	9	5	9	7	9	5	9	3
♓	6	7	6	10	6	8	7	9	8	6	4	10

1 = the pits
10 = the peaks

Key

♈ - Aries
♉ - Taurus
♊ - Gemini
♋ - Cancer
♌ - Leo
♍ - Virgo

♎ - Libra
♏ - Scorpio
♐ - Sagittarius
♑ - Capricorn
♒ - Aquarius
♓ - Pisces

YOUR POTENTIAL AND CREATIVITY

Have you ever wondered if you're living up to your Sun sign's potential? Have you been curious to know if you have other skills that you've yet to explore? Do you feel as though something is missing from your life? If you've answered 'yes' to any of these questions, read on to discover how to make the best of your Sun sign.

Virgo

You have a marvellous eye for detail, good manual dexterity and astonishing reserves of patience, so you might enjoy doing something that draws on these talents. You could develop a passion for jigsaws, for instance! If you want to do something practical, perhaps even that you can sell to make some money, how about teaching yourself a very fiddly skill such as lace-making, découpage, mosaics or embroidery? With your interest in health matters and your Virgoan need to serve others, you might consider taking up medicine professionally. If you feel it's too late to train to be a doctor or nurse, how about learning chiropody or one of the complementary therapies? If you prefer to do something with figures, you could consider taking a course in higher mathematics or accountancy. Very useful!

Libra

You belong to one of the two most attractive signs of all, so you might enjoy making the most of it! For instance, you could decide to learn a beauty therapy or anything else that makes people feel good. Training to be an aromatherapist or masseur could appeal to you. You enjoy the sensual feel of natural fabrics such as velvet and silk, so how about doing some dressmaking? You might become so good at it that you end up making clothes for other people as well – and being paid for it! Don't overlook your diplomatic skills either. If you were considering doing some voluntary work, for instance, you might be excellent working on a phoneline or doing some sort of counselling. You would easily be able to combine compassion with objectivity.

Scorpio

You store so many of your experiences deep inside you that it's important to find constructive and creative outlets for them. Writing down your thoughts in a diary is one option, or maybe you'd prefer to do something rather more dramatic, such as performing poetry? As a Scorpio you are naturally attuned to the areas in life that many of us shy away from, so you could gain tremendous fulfilment from becoming a bereavement counsellor, working with people who have Aids or being a volunteer in a hospice. You would have the satisfaction of knowing you were doing something truly valuable. On a lighter note, many Scorpios are wine buffs, so how about going on a wine tasting course or teaching yourself to appreciate wine? Think of the fun you'd have!

Sagittarius

You have such an open mind that you're always interested in finding new ways to express yourself. You've probably already worked your way through a string of different interests and you know there are plenty more where those came from. If you're stuck for ideas, how about developing something that's already a theme in your life? If you enjoy travel, you might decide to learn a foreign language. It will give you a big kick to go abroad and chat away to the locals in their own tongue. If you're interested in history, you might decide to study a particular period in great detail, or collect items that date from that period. Activities that improve the environment may also appeal to you, and you might even end up getting involved in politics!

Capricorn

Have you ever thought of rock climbing? After all, you do belong to the sign of the mountain goat! Even if you can't bear the thought of dangling off a cliff face, you might like the idea of doing some hill walking or rambling. They'd be good antidotes to all those hours you spend at work. Alternatively, if you're looking for an unusual pet, how about keeping a goat? Any activities that help you to express your reliability are good for you, although you must make sure you aren't saddled with all the tasks that no one else wants to do. You might consider learning accountancy so that you can sort out your own finances and those of your friends, or learning the intricacies of the stock market so you can start making some clever investments.

Aquarius

If you're currently wondering how to give your life more meaning, have you considered doing something that brings out your humanitarian streak? You have a very rational view of the world that deserves a wider audience. You might get involved in a charity by giving regular donations, or you could decide to lend a hand in other ways, such as volunteering your time. Alternatively, you could be interested in politics, especially if you get fed up shouting at the television when you hear about things you don't agree with. You could soon be shouting at fellow councillors or MPs! If you're fascinated by outer space, how about buying yourself a telescope and a star map? You'll also love learning about the science of astronomy. Watching a science fiction film will never be the same again!

Pisces

If you're looking for new ways to express your Piscean talents, swimming is something that might appeal. Surprisingly, given that this is the sign of the fish, many Pisceans aren't very good at swimming, so you could combine swimming lessons with regular exercise. Dance is another Piscean activity, whether you're doing the dancing or watching someone else. It's certainly very important for you to do something that allows you to express yourself, otherwise you'll feel stifled and unfulfilled. You might be interested in learning aromatherapy or working with crystals, and your powerful intuition could make you a natural tarot reader or caster of the runes. You'll also enjoy the slightly mysterious aspects of it all.

Aries

Two of your greatest strengths are your fiery enthusiasm and your enjoyment in being a daredevil. You don't want to stand on the sidelines when you could be right in the thick of things. Even if you aren't really risking life and limb, you like to imagine that you are. Any activity that brings excitement into your life and appeals to your intrepid spirit will suit you well. How about rock climbing, hang-gliding or bungee jumping? They'll all get the adrenalin flowing! You're also ace at sports and athletics, so you might decide to show off your skills on the football or rugby pitch. Being an explorer also appeals to you, so you'll get a real buzz from being the first in your social circle to do something new. With luck, you'll start a trend!

Taurus

Any activity that draws on your resolute character and your practical nature will bring out the best in you. You're also extremely artistic so will enjoy expressing your creative talents. Anything that brings you into contact with the great outdoors is perfect for you. For instance, gardening might be an ideal occupation for you. You thoroughly enjoy working with nature, and being out in the fresh air helps you to clear your head and get problems in perspective. Taurus is the sign that rules beautiful voices, so how about taking singing lessons? Even if you think you can't sing a note, you'll really enjoy discovering your natural voice and using it as a vehicle for self-expression. If you have a sweet tooth, you may also enjoy making your own chocolates. But don't be surprised if you're deluged with requests from friends!

Gemini

Anything that allows you to communicate is right up your street. If you've always toyed with the idea of writing a novel or becoming a journalist but have never done anything about it, it isn't too late to start! Even keeping a regular journal will encourage you to put your thoughts down on paper and you'll soon find it becomes second nature. Who knows where it might lead! Geminis are noted for their ability to think quickly and analytically, so you might enjoy teaching yourself how to do logic puzzles or cryptic crosswords. Or maybe you'd enjoy showing off your range of knowledge in a pub quiz? This is the sign that rules the hands, so if you're looking for a sideline you might consider training to be a manicurist – or maybe you'd like to teach yourself palmistry!

Cancer

You belong to the sign of the homemaker, so anything that will improve the atmosphere or appearance of your home is a natural choice for you. You might decide to learn how to make soft furnishings, you could stitch a needlepoint cushion or even a rug if you're feeling ambitious, or you could train to be an interior decorator. Cancerians are often fascinated by the past, so you might decide to research your family tree or organize all the family photographs into chronological order. If you want to take this one step further, how about signing up for a history course or taking a class in antiques? Cooking is another wonderful way for you to express yourself, and if you're good at it you can expect lots of encouragement from your family and friends!

Leo

You have a head start because you belong to one of the most creative signs of all. If you've always fancied treading the boards but have never fancied it as a career, you might consider joining an amateur dramatics group. It might satisfy your instinctive Leo yearning to be in the limelight. Alternatively, how about joining a poetry circle or writing group in which you can perform your work? Many Leos are born artists, so you might be interested in learning how to paint or draw. Or perhaps you'd like to do something slightly different, such as painting silk scarves or making stained-glass windows or jewellery? You can also find it inspiring to put your terrific organizational skills to good use.

BORN ON THE CUSP?

Were you born on the cusp of Virgo – at the beginning or end of the sign? If so, you may have spent years wondering which sign you belong to. Are you a Virgo, a Leo or a Libran? Different horoscope books and columns can give different dates for when the Sun moves into each sign, leaving you utterly confused. Yet none of these dates is wrong, as you'll discover in a minute. Checking your birth date, and time if you know it, in the list given in this chapter will allow you to solve the mystery at long last!

Many people believe that the Sun moves like clockwork from one sign to another on a specific day each year. But this isn't always true. For instance, let's look at the dates for the sign of Virgo. On the cover of this book I give them as 24 August to 23 September. Very often, the Sun will obediently change signs on these days but sometimes it won't. It can move from Leo into Virgo on 22, 23 or 24 August and it can move into Libra on 22, 23 or 24 September.

So how can you find out which sign you belong to if you were born on the cusp of Virgo? The only information you need is the place, year, day and the time of your birth if you know it. It helps to have the time of birth because if the Sun did move signs on your birthday, you can see whether it moved before or after you were born. If you don't have an exact time, even knowing whether it was morning or afternoon can be a help. For instance, if you were born in the morning and the Sun didn't move signs on your birthday until the afternoon, that will be enough information to tell you which sign is yours.

You need to know the place in case you were born outside the United Kingdom and have to convert its local time zone to British time. This information is easily available in many diaries and reference books.

Four Simple Steps to Find your Sun Sign

1. Write down the year, day, time and place of your birth, in that order.
2. If you were born outside the United Kingdom, you must convert your birth date and time to British time by adding or subtracting the relevant number of hours from your birth time to convert it to British time. This may take your birthday into the following day or back to the previous day. If so, write down this new date and time because that will be the one you use in the following calculations. If summer time was operating you must deduct the relevant number of hours to convert your birth time to Greenwich Mean Time (GMT).
3. If you were born in Britain, look up your year of birth in the list of British Summer Time (BST) changes to see if BST was operating when you were born. If it was, subtract the appropriate number of hours from your birth time to convert it to GMT. This may give you a different time and/or date of birth.
4. Look up your year of birth in the Annual Sun Sign Changes list. If you were born within these dates and times, you are a Virgo. If you were born outside them, you are either a Leo if you were born in August, or a Libran if you were born in September.

Two Examples

Here are a couple of examples so you can see how the process works. Let's say we're looking for the Sun sign of Bob, who was born in the UK on 24 August 1944 at 01:30. Start by checking the list of British Summer Time dates to see if BST was operating at the time of his birth. It was, but you will see that he was born during a phase when two hours had been added, so you have to subtract two hours from his birth time to convert it to GMT. This gives him a birth time of 23:30 on the previous day – therefore, his GMT birthday is 23 August and his GMT birth time is 23:30. Write this down, so you don't forget it. Now turn to the Annual Sun Sign Changes list and look for 1944, his year of birth. In that year, the Sun moved into Virgo on 23 August at 06:47, and Bob's GMT birth time was at 23:30 that day, so he is a Virgo. However, if he had been born on 23 August 1944 at 01:30 (which gives him a GMT birth time of 23:30 on 22 August), the Sun would have been in Leo so he would be a Leo.

But what would his sign be if he were born on 23 September 1944 at 13:30? First check the dates in the BST list for 1944. You will see he was born during a period when one hour had been added for BST, so you must subtract one hour to convert his birth time to GMT. This changes it to 12:30 on 23 September 1944. Write this down. Now look up the Sun sign dates for 1944. Look at the September date. The Sun was in Virgo until 23 September at 04:01. So Bob's GMT birth time was after the Sun had moved into Libra, making him a Libran.

Dates for British Summer Time

If your birthday falls within these dates and times, you were born during BST and will have to convert your birth time back to GMT. To do this, subtract one hour from your birth time. If you were born during a period that is marked *, you must subtract two hours from your birth time to convert it to GMT. All times are given in BST, using the 24-hour clock.

1920 28 Mar, 02:00–25 Oct, 01:59 inc
1921 3 Apr, 02:00–3 Oct, 01:59 inc
1922 26 Mar, 02:00–8 Oct, 01:59 inc
1923 22 Apr, 02:00–16 Sep, 01:59 inc
1924 13 Apr, 02:00–21 Sep, 01:59 inc
1925 19 Apr, 02:00–4 Oct, 01:59 inc
1926 18 Apr, 02:00–3 Oct, 01:59 inc
1927 10 Apr, 02:00–2 Oct, 01:59 inc
1928 22 Apr, 02:00–7 Oct, 01:59 inc
1929 21 Apr, 02:00–6 Oct, 01:59 inc
1930 13 Apr, 02:00–5 Oct, 01:59 inc
1931 19 Apr, 02:00–4 Oct, 01:59 inc
1932 17 Apr, 02:00–2 Oct, 01:59 inc
1933 9 Apr, 02:00–8 Oct, 01:59 inc
1934 22 Apr, 02:00–7 Oct, 01:59 inc
1935 14 Apr, 02:00–6 Oct, 01:59 inc
1936 19 Apr, 02:00–4 Oct, 01:59 inc
1937 18 Apr, 02:00–3 Oct, 01:59 inc
1938 10 Apr, 02:00–2 Oct, 01:59 inc
1939 16 Apr, 02:00–19 Nov, 01:59 inc
1940 25 Feb, 02:00–31 Dec, 23:59 inc
1941 1 Jan, 00:00–4 May, 01:59 inc
1941 4 May, 02:00–10 Aug, 01:59 inc*
1941 10 Aug, 02:00–31 Dec, 23:59 inc
1942 1 Jan, 00:00–5 Apr, 01:59 inc
1942 5 Apr, 02:00–9 Aug, 01:59 inc*
1942 9 Aug, 02:00–31 Dec, 23:59 inc
1943 1 Jan, 00:00–4 Apr, 01:59 inc
1943 4 Apr, 02:00–15 Aug, 01:59 inc*
1943 15 Aug, 02:00–31 Dec, 23:59 inc
1944 1 Jan, 00:00–2 Apr, 01:59 inc
1944 2 Apr, 02:00–17 Sep, 01:59 inc*
1944 17 Sep, 02:00–31 Dec, 23:59 inc
1945 1 Jan, 02:00–2 Apr, 01:59 inc
1945 2 Apr, 02:00–15 Jul, 01:59 inc*
1945 15 Jul, 02:00–7 Oct, 01:59 inc
1946 14 Apr, 02:00–6 Oct, 01:59 inc
1947 16 Mar, 02:00–13 Apr, 01:59 inc
1947 13 Apr, 02:00–10 Aug, 01:59 inc*
1947 10 Aug, 02:00–2 Nov, 01:59 inc
1948 14 Mar, 02:00–31 Oct, 01:59 inc
1949 3 Apr, 02:00–30 Oct, 01:59 inc
1950 16 Apr, 02:00–22 Oct, 01:59 inc
1951 15 Apr, 02:00–21 Oct, 01:59 inc
1952 20 Apr, 02:00–26 Oct, 01:59 inc
1953 19 Apr, 02:00–4 Oct, 01:59 inc
1954 11 Apr, 02:00–3 Oct, 01:59 inc
1955 17 Apr, 02:00–2 Oct, 01:59 inc
1956 22 Apr, 02:00–7 Oct, 01:59 inc
1957 14 Apr, 02:00–6 Oct, 01:59 inc
1958 20 Apr, 02:00–5 Oct, 01:59 inc
1959 19 Apr, 02:00–4 Oct, 01:59 inc
1960 10 Apr, 02:00–2 Oct, 01:59 inc
1961 26 Mar, 02:00–29 Oct, 01:59 inc
1962 25 Mar, 02:00–28 Oct, 01:59 inc
1963 31 Mar, 02:00–27 Oct, 01:59 inc
1964 22 Mar, 02:00–25 Oct, 01:59 inc
1965 21 Mar, 02:00–24 Oct, 01:59 inc
1966 20 Mar, 02:00–23 Oct, 01:59 inc
1967 19 Mar, 02:00–29 Oct, 01:59 inc
1968 18 Feb, 02:00–31 Dec, 23:59 inc
1969 1 Jan, 00:00–31 Dec, 23:59 inc
1970 1 Jan, 00:00–31 Dec, 23:59 inc
1971 1 Jan, 00:00–31 Oct, 01:59 inc
1972 19 Mar, 02:00–29 Oct, 01:59 inc
1973 18 Mar, 02:00–28 Oct, 01:59 inc
1974 17 Mar, 02:00–27 Oct, 01:59 inc
1975 16 Mar, 02:00–26 Oct, 01:59 inc
1976 21 Mar, 02:00–24 Oct, 01:59 inc
1977 20 Mar, 02:00–23 Oct, 01:59 inc
1978 19 Mar, 02:00–29 Oct, 01:59 inc
1979 18 Mar, 02:00–28 Oct, 01:59 inc
1980 16 Mar, 02:00–26 Oct, 01:59 inc
1981 29 Mar, 01:00–25 Oct, 00:59 inc
1982 28 Mar, 01:00–24 Oct, 00:59 inc
1983 27 Mar, 01:00–23 Oct, 00:59 inc
1984 25 Mar, 01:00–28 Oct, 00:59 inc
1985 31 Mar, 01:00–27 Oct, 00:59 inc
1986 30 Mar, 01:00–26 Oct, 00:59 inc
1987 29 Mar, 01:00–25 Oct, 00:59 inc
1988 27 Mar, 01:00–23 Oct, 00:59 inc
1989 26 Mar, 01:00–29 Oct, 00:59 inc
1990 25 Mar, 01:00–28 Oct, 00:59 inc
1991 31 Mar, 01:00–27 Oct, 00:59 inc
1992 29 Mar, 01:00–25 Oct, 00:59 inc
1993 28 Mar, 01:00–24 Oct, 00:59 inc

1994 27 Mar, 01:00–23 Oct, 00:59 inc
1995 26 Mar, 01:00–22 Oct, 00:59 inc
1996 31 Mar, 01:00–27 Oct, 00:59 inc
1997 30 Mar, 01:00–26 Oct, 00:59 inc
1998 29 Mar, 01:00–25 Oct, 00:59 inc
1999 28 Mar, 01:00–31 Oct, 00:59 inc
2000 26 Mar, 01:00–29 Oct, 00:59 inc
2001 25 Mar, 01:00–28 Oct, 00:59 inc
2002 24 Mar, 01:00–27 Oct, 00:59 inc

* Subtract two hours from the birth time to convert it to GMT.

Annual Sun Sign Changes

If your birthday falls within these dates and times, you are a Virgo. If you were born in August before the first date and time, you are a Leo. If you were born in September after the second date and time, you are a Libran. All times are given in GMT, using the 24-hour clock.

1920 23 Aug, 11:22–23 Sep, 08:28 inc
1921 23 Aug, 17:16–23 Sep, 14:19 inc
1922 23 Aug, 23:05–23 Sep, 20:09 inc
1923 24 Aug, 04:52–24 Sep, 02:03 inc
1924 23 Aug, 10:48–23 Sep, 07:58 inc
1925 23 Aug, 16:34–23 Sep, 13:43 inc
1926 23 Aug, 22:14–23 Sep, 19:26 inc
1927 24 Aug, 04:06–24 Sep, 01:16 inc
1928 23 Aug, 09:54–23 Sep, 07:05 inc
1929 23 Aug, 15:42–23 Sep, 12:52 inc
1930 23 Aug, 21:27–23 Sep, 18:35 inc
1931 24 Aug, 03:11–24 Sep, 00:23 inc
1932 23 Aug, 09:07–23 Sep, 06:15 inc
1933 23 Aug, 14:53–23 Sep, 12:01 inc
1934 23 Aug, 20:32–23 Sep, 17:45 inc
1935 24 Aug, 02:24–23 Sep, 23:38 inc
1936 23 Aug, 08:11–23 Sep, 05:25 inc
1937 23 Aug, 13:58–23 Sep, 11:12 inc
1938 23 Aug, 19:46–23 Sep, 16:59 inc
1939 24 Aug, 01:32–23 Sep, 22:49 inc
1940 23 Aug, 07:29–23 Sep, 04:45 inc
1941 23 Aug, 13:17–23 Sep, 10:32 inc
1942 23 Aug, 18:59–23 Sep, 16:16 inc
1943 24 Aug, 00:55–23 Sep, 22:11 inc
1944 23 Aug, 06:47–23 Sep, 04:01 inc
1945 23 Aug, 12:36–23 Sep, 09:49 inc
1946 23 Aug, 18:27–23 Sep, 15:40 inc
1947 24 Aug, 00:09–23 Sep, 21:28 inc
1948 23 Aug, 06:03–23 Sep, 03:21 inc
1949 23 Aug, 11:49–23 Sep, 09:05 inc
1950 23 Aug, 17:24–23 Sep, 14:43 inc
1951 23 Aug, 23:17–23 Sep, 20:36 inc
1952 23 Aug, 05:03–23 Sep, 02:23 inc
1953 23 Aug, 10:46–23 Sep, 08:05 inc
1954 23 Aug, 16:36–23 Sep, 13:55 inc
1955 23 Aug, 22:19–23 Sep, 19:40 inc
1956 23 Aug, 04:15–23 Sep, 01:35 inc
1957 23 Aug, 10:08–23 Sep, 07:26 inc
1958 23 Aug, 15:46–23 Sep, 13:08 inc
1959 23 Aug, 21:44–23 Sep, 19:08 inc
1960 23 Aug, 03:35–23 Sep, 00:58 inc
1961 23 Aug, 09:19–23 Sep, 06:42 inc
1962 23 Aug, 15:13–23 Sep, 12:35 inc
1963 23 Aug, 20:58–23 Sep, 18:23 inc
1964 23 Aug, 02:52–23 Sep, 00:16 inc
1965 23 Aug, 08:43–23 Sep, 06:06 inc
1966 23 Aug, 14:18–23 Sep, 11:43 inc
1967 23 Aug, 20:13–23 Sep, 17:38 inc
1968 23 Aug, 02:04–22 Sep, 23:26 inc
1969 23 Aug, 07:44–23 Sep, 05:07 inc
1970 23 Aug, 13:35–23 Sep, 10:59 inc
1971 23 Aug, 19:16–23 Sep, 16:45 inc
1972 23 Aug, 01:04–22 Sep, 22:32 inc
1973 23 Aug, 06:54–23 Sep, 04:21 inc

1974 23 Aug, 12:29–23 Sep, 09:58 inc
1975 23 Aug, 18:24–23 Sep, 15:55 inc
1976 23 Aug, 00:19–22 Sep, 21:48 inc
1977 23 Aug, 06:01–23 Sep, 03:29 inc
1978 23 Aug, 11:58–23 Sep, 09:25 inc
1979 23 Aug, 17:48–23 Sep, 15:16 inc
1980 22 Aug, 23:42–22 Sep, 21:09 inc
1981 23 Aug, 05:39–23 Sep, 03:05 inc
1982 23 Aug, 11:16–23 Sep, 08:46 inc
1983 23 Aug, 17:08–23 Sep, 14:42 inc
1984 22 Aug, 23:01–22 Sep, 20:33 inc
1985 23 Aug, 04:37–23 Sep, 02:07 inc
1986 23 Aug, 10:27–23 Sep, 07:59 inc
1987 23 Aug, 16:11–23 Sep, 13:45 inc
1988 22 Aug, 21:55–22 Sep, 19:29 inc
1989 23 Aug, 03:47–23 Sep, 01:20 inc
1990 23 Aug, 09:22–23 Sep, 06:55 inc
1991 23 Aug, 15:14–23 Sep, 12:48 inc
1992 22 Aug, 21:11–22 Sep, 18:43 inc
1993 23 Aug, 02:51–23 Sep, 00:22 inc
1994 23 Aug, 08:45–23 Sep, 06:19 inc
1995 23 Aug, 14:36–23 Sep, 12:13 inc
1996 22 Aug, 20:24–22 Sep, 18:00 inc
1997 23 Aug, 02:20–22 Sep, 23:56 inc
1998 23 Aug, 08:00–23 Sep, 05:37 inc
1999 23 Aug, 13:52–23 Sep, 11:32 inc
2000 22 Aug, 19:50–22 Sep, 17:28 inc
2001 23 Aug, 01:28–22 Sep, 23:05 inc
2002 23 Aug, 07:18–23 Sep, 04:55 inc